Hill Walkers Wicklow

30 One-Day Walking Routes in the Mountains near Dublin

David Herman

SHANKSMARE PUBLICATIONS

"Since men almost always tread the paths made by others, and proceed in their affairs by imitation, although they are not completely able to stay on the path of others, or attain the skill of those they imitate, a prudent man should always enter those paths taken by great men and imitate those who have been most excellent..."

...(Machiavelli's The Prince, Chapter VI).

WICKLOW

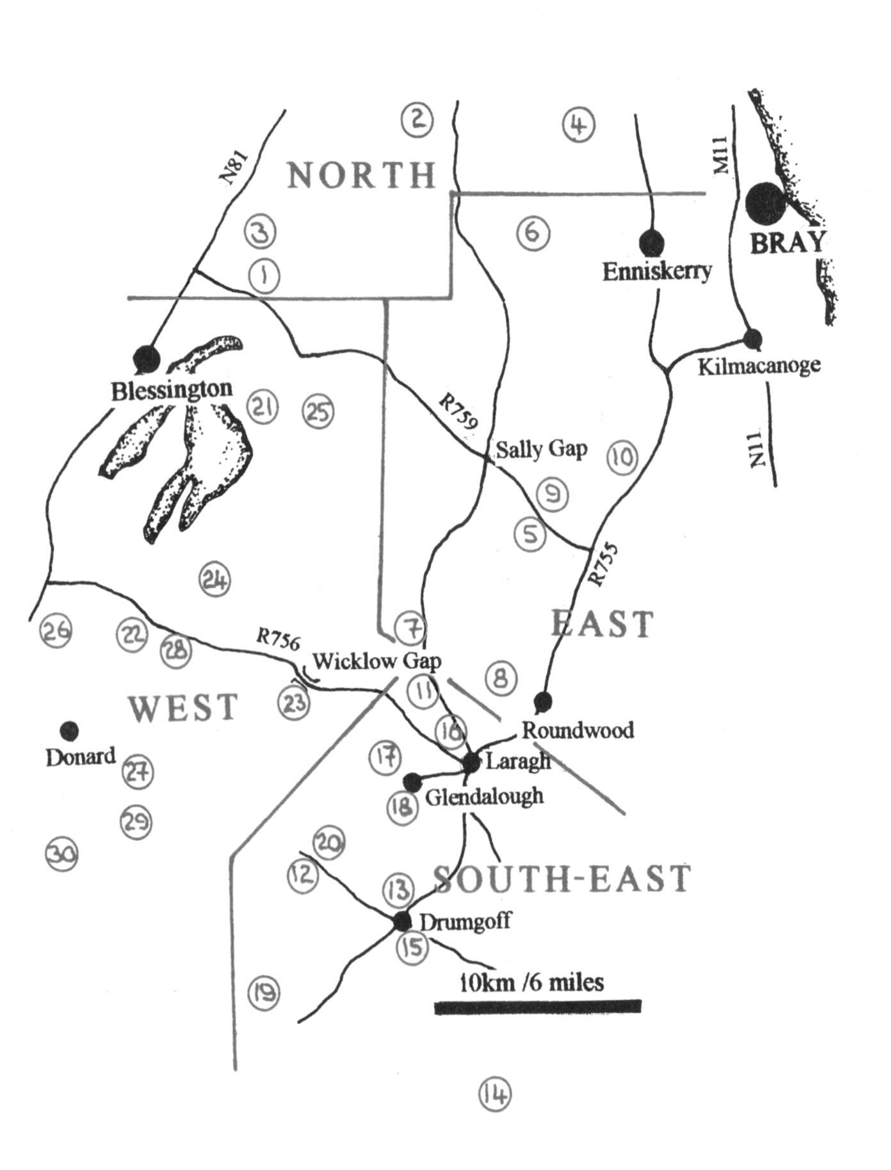

NORTH
EAST
WEST
SOUTH-EAST
N81
M11
N11
R759
R755
R756
BRAY
Enniskerry
Kilmacanoge
Blessington
Sally Gap
Wicklow Gap
Roundwood
Laragh
Glendalough
Donard
Drumgoff
10km /6 miles
1
2
3
4
5
6
7
8
9
10
11
12
13
14
15
16
17
18
19
20
21
22
23
24
25
26
27
28
29
30

CONTENTS

* Routes with Major Variations

INTRODUCTION: WHAT'S NEW

This is the third edition of this book; as in the past I have tried to vary the routes from the previous edition. This is for two main reasons. The first is obvious: if you have bought one of the previous editions of this book you might consider buying this one if it contains something new. Less obviously, except to anyone who has come back to the Wicklow Mountains after an interval of ten or even five years, is the great increase in the number of walkers and the consequent increase in erosion. We must all do our part in reducing erosion. While you might argue that one way would be not to publish guide books, what I have done in this edition is to try to avoid particularly eroded sections of routes. If you see that the route I give differs from what is the direct route on the map, this is probably the reason.

To get back to the point about guide books: if we had no books, and to go further no maps, the result would probably be that walkers would stick to the most popular and therefore the most eroded routes; there would be only a marginal effect on the numbers walking or on the total amount of erosion. At least with guide books the burden on the mountains is spread a little and walkers might consider venturing into areas that they do not know.

What is new in the mountains since the last edition in 1997? The Wicklow Mountains National Park has attained almost its full extent, and how welcome it is. As I have done in the last edition I ask you to support the work of the Park in any way you can. In particular, and this is surely a sign of the times, the Park authorities have built boardwalks on some stretches of eroded paths. Keep to them.

The only other major development is the publication of a new 1:25 000 map of part of the mountains; it shows forests and forest tracks more accurately than the OS maps. There is more about maps below.

A QUICK LOOK AROUND

Dubliners are lucky to have on their doorsteps the largest area of upland in Ireland, an area encompassing some fine peaks, beautiful mountain valleys cradling lovely lakes and vast (maybe too vast) areas of moorland.

Let's first look briefly at the whole of the mountain area by describing the four regions into which the book is divided. The exact boundaries of these regions are shown on the key map.

The North (routes 1-4), the area nearest Dublin, is greatly influenced by the city itself. This proximity has some advantages but more disadvantages. The main advantage is that it is easy to access, with public transport reaching some fairly good mountain areas. The main disadvantages stem from this proximity: masts of all types, litter, and overcrowded and eroded paths and tracks. The terrain itself consists mostly of gently rounded peaks and shoulders, the city and coastline in view from the north-east corner, and the area further west offering a more remote ambience.

The East (routes 5-11) encompasses some of the most attractive scenery in Wicklow, though unfortunately – and indeed consequently – there are a few badly eroded areas. Djouce (routes 6, 9, 10) is the highest peak while the area round two large mountain lakes, Tay and Dan (routes 6-9), which are partly surrounded by fine peaks, offers particularly memorable walking. Further west beyond the

Military Road the spine of the range runs through the second and third highest peaks in the Wicklow mountains, Mullaghcleevaun (849m) (routes 24, 25 below) and Tonelagee (817m), an especially fine mountain (route 11 and 16 below).

The South-East (routes 12-20) is focused around two well-known and scenic valleys. Glendalough is a glacial valley with strong historical associations and is almost surrounded by distinctive peaks (routes 16-18). It is a deservedly popular centre for walking and has a modest though invaluable bus service from Dublin. Further south is Glenmalure, another good centre for walking (routes 12, 13, 15, 20). Overlooking Glenmalure is the Lugnaquillia massif, culminating in Lugnaquillia itself (925m). This is a high-level area with some lovely peaks, mountain valleys, cliffs and corries (routes 12, 19 and also routes 27 and 29 below). To the south the mountain country is diversified by agricultural land and some forestry (route 14).

The West (routes 21-30) is dominated on the north by the large expanse of Pollaphuca Reservoir, a pleasant body of water which enhances the views from the otherwise none too inspiring peaks around it (routes 21, 24-26). Directly south of the R756 road (routes 22, 23, 28) is some of the most desolate country in Wicklow (this is not necessarily a condemnation!). Further south lies the almost circular basin of the Glen of Imaal (routes 27, 29, 30), which is backed on the north by some good, though rounded peaks and on the east by the impressive Lugnaquillia massif (see above).

HOW TO USE THIS BOOK

First of all, you would be better off with OS maps rather than relying on the extracts from those maps given in this book. More about suitable maps is given below and with each route description.

I have tried to cover all the best and most characteristic of the mountain areas of counties Wicklow and Dublin – of course the best are not necessarily the most characteristic. In doing so, I have not described every area covered by every route in superlative terms. All the routes chosen have some favourable characteristics and some, and only some, have unfavourable ones. These judgements are just that – judgements – and you might well have quite different verdicts.

The Maps The extract from the full-colour Ordnance Survey (OS) 1:50 000 maps that accompanies each route description is obviously not as useful as the original maps. They will however get you round the route assuming you do not stray too far, *but usually do not cover the variations.* The extracts are supplemented in red by the route and by symbols indicating features that are missing from the original maps. These symbols are explained on the inside back cover. Remember that the side of each square on the extracts represents 1km and that if you are taking grid bearings from the extracts add 8° to get compass bearings.

Walking Time This is based on 4km/hr on the flat and a climbing rate of 500m/hr, so that a walk of 4km with a climb of 250m should take 1 hours. This is a fairly leisurely pace and if you are reasonably fit you should have no difficulty in keeping to it. The time is adjusted for difficult conditions (eg high vegetation, steep *descents*) or good (eg clear tracks) and in these instances the adjustment is noted in the text.

Metric versus Imperial Metric units are used throughout - if you simply can't think metric you can use the tables on the inside back cover. The one occasion where imperial units are used is where cars are involved, as they are usually equipped with milometers.
Grid References These are the four or six digit numbers, preceded by the letters 'GR' which appear in this book after some locations, particularly the start of routes. The figure uniquely identifies the location. The system is explained on all OS maps.
Warning Things change, even the 'eternal hills'. Of all the mountain ranges in Ireland, Wicklow is probably the one most subject to change. New forest tracks are constructed, there are many areas of fast-growing trees, houses are built across paths and areas which were accessible turn overnight into a nightmare of intimidating fences. Please bear in mind that if the route description does not make sense it is not necessarily the author's fault. It could be that there is a new feature in the landscape or that a feature that I describe has disappeared. For the record, with only a few minor exceptions, every section of every route was walked not earlier than spring 1999.

ACCESSING THE MOUNTAINS FROM DUBLIN

I must first apologize for assuming that you will always travel from Dublin to the mountains. However, most hill walkers in these mountains do come from Dublin and it is the one large centre from which all parts of the mountains are best accessed.

By Car

Getting to the mountains from Dublin is not easy mainly because of inadequate sign-posting. The method used here is to use 'jumping-off' points. For each route first drive from Dublin to the appropriate jumping-off point (indicated in *italics* in the paragraph 'Getting There' in the route description). From there drive to the starting point as indicated in the same paragraph.

Here are the jumping-off points (the figures in brackets given after each represents miles from central Dublin):
Blessington (18): Drive through Harold's Cross, Terenure and Templeogue following signs for the N81.
Donard (31) (GR 9397): Follow signs for the N81, turning left (signposted) about 11 miles south of Blessington.
Drumgoff crossroads (Glenmalure) (36) (GR 1090): Drive to *Laragh* (see below), continue on the R755 for about 1 mile. Fork right (signed 'Glenmalure') for Drumgoff crossroads, which is about $4^1/_2$ miles further on.
Enniskerry (13): Follow signs for Ranelagh and Dundrum, then continue straight ahead on the R117.
Glenasmole (9) (GR 0922): Follow signs for Rathfarnham on the R114, turn right at the traffic lights at Rathfarnham Castle onto Butterfield Avenue to stay on the R114. Continue straight ahead on the R114 for 5.7 miles, turning left here (unsigned) into Glenasmole.
Glendalough (31), *Laragh* (30): Follow signs for the M11/N11 initially through Leeson Street and Donnybrook. Turn right onto the R755 at Kilmacanoge.

Lackan (22) (GR 0111): Follow signs for the N81 to *Blessington*, turn left after Downshire Hotel, turn right shortly over the reservoir, turn right immediately at the tee, continue on the main road to the village.
Rockbrook (6) (GR 1324): Follow signs for Rathfarnham, pass Rathfarnham Castle (on left), turn right immediately after at the Yellow House pub (on right). Continue straight ahead for about $2^1/_2$ miles to the village.
Roundwood (26) (GR 1903): Follow signs for the M11/N11 initially through Leeson Street and Donnybrook; turn right onto the R755 at Kilmacanoge.
Sally Gap (17) (GR 1311), *Military Road*: Take the N81 to Terenure, continue straight ahead to pass Rathfarnham Castle (on left), turn right immediately after at the Yellow House pub (on right). After 1.2 miles go straight ahead at a roundabout but take the next right onto Scholarstown Road. Take the second left almost immediately onto Stocking Lane and continue straight ahead.
Wicklow Gap (35) (GR 0700): can be reached from *Glendalough* by forking right just before the village or by taking the N81 through *Blessington* and then the R756.
A Word of Caution to Travellers by Car There have been many thefts in recent years from cars parked in mountain locations. It is therefore advisable never to leave valuables in unattended cars. Do *not* leave a note visible in your car indicating when you intend to arrive back.

By Bus

The following Dublin Bus services (☎ 01-873 4222) may be useful.

For the north-west corner of the mountains note the services 47 (Tibradden (GR 149253), infrequent), 47A (Rockbrook (GR 137247), moderately frequent), 47B (Grange Road (GR 160257), moderately frequent), 203 (Bohernabreena (GR 096245), frequent).

For Barnacullia (GR 1823), Glencullen (GR 1820), note the 44B service (infrequent).

For the north-east corner note the services 44 (Enniskerry, frequent), and the Shop River variation of the 85 which travels 2.5km west of Enniskerry (fairly frequent).

For the west (N81) note the 65 to Blessington (frequent), Ballymore Eustace, Ballyknockan and Donard (all very infrequent).

There is a very useful service along the east of the range terminating in Glendalough. This is the St Kevin's Bus (☎ 01-281 8119) which runs from St Stephen's Green in Dublin through Kilmacanoge, Roundwood and Laragh to Glendalough. The service is fairly infrequent. Reid's Buses (☎ 0404-67671) runs a regular service between Wicklow town and Glendalough.

There are two Irish Bus / Bus Eireann express services (limited stops) that might be of some use. They are the table 2 with a service from Dublin along the east of the range and table 5 with services along both the east and west of the range. There are also two Irish Bus local services (ie buses which stop anywhere as long as it is safe to do so) which also might be useful. They are table 132 (very infrequent) which runs along the west of the range with a useful stop at Annalecky Cross (GR 9199) near Donard, and timetable 133 (fairly frequent) which runs along the east of the range.

MAPS

The whole of the mountain area is adequately covered by the OS Discovery Series on a scale of 1:50 000 with 10m contour interval. (As explained above the map extracts given in this book are taken from this Series.) Sheet 50 covers roughly the mountains near Dublin and sheet 62 the very south of the range. Sheet 56 covers the bulk of the mountain area and is thus a well worthwhile investment. There is no overlap between sheets, so both text and map extracts given in this book give compass bearings to cover the more awkward transitions between sheets.

Since most hill walkers will use this series it is worthwhile considering some of its limitations:

- Cliffs are not depicted explicitly on the maps, though they are shown on the map extracts given here.
- The extent of forestry planting has generally been exaggerated.
- Forest tracks are badly depicted, with many clear tracks omitted and others shown where they do not exist. 'Forest tracks' on the map that run up hill and down dale regardless of the terrain are generally firebreaks.
- The route of the Wicklow Way is badly shown.
- Footpaths and footbridges are generally omitted.
- Some streams in upland areas are depicted by formidably thick lines; nevertheless you can assume that they are normally fordable (the route descriptions in this book will alert you to streams that may be difficult to ford). The courses of other streams are totally obliterated by the National Park boundary line.

The National Parks have published a map of the Glendalough area on a scale of 1:25 000 with a 15m contour interval. It covers a small but popular area and is particularly good in its depiction of tracks and paths. It may be obtained at the Visitor Centre in Glendalough.

There is a 1:25 000 map covering the central mountain area south-west of Lough Dan and including the Lugnaquillia area, Glendalough and Glenmalure. It shows forest tracks far more accurately than the OS maps and indicates cliffs explicitly as well as showing minor but useful features such as fences and rock areas. Entitled 'Glendalough Glenmalur' it is on sale in bookshops or may be obtained from Pat Healy, Cut Bush, The Curragh, Co Kildare (fax/☎ 045-41625).

A guide and strip map on a scale of 1:50 000 covering the route of the Wicklow Way is published by EastWest Mapping (☎ 054-77835). It is useful for the limited area on the east of the range that it covers because it shows forest tracks and paths correctly, as noted above a major failing with OS maps.

Lastly, there is the 1:126 720 (half-inch to the mile) OS sheet 16, which covers almost the entire mountain area and much more besides. Its scale is far too small and it is out of date and therefore of little use except for giving an overall view of the mountain area and its environs.

SAFETY

Before you start out It is essential to leave your intended route with someone; to have a map and compass and to know how to use them; to wear proper walking boots and carry raingear. It's advisable that at least three walk together. Get a weather forecast before you go.

On the Walk Do not press on regardless in the face of worsening weather or falling night. Remember that the major factor by far affecting route finding in the mountains is visibility. Cloud and fog make all the difference to navigation. As well as the obvious lack of visibility they are disorienting and distorting, so that what is in reality a minor hill near at hand will appear through cloud like a major mountain much further away. In such inauspicious conditions, try to find out exactly where you are before visibility fails. Pay careful attention to your route and time your progress using Naismith's Rule.

If You Get Lost First, think. A few minutes thought may save hours of blundering around in the dark or in cloud. You must have some idea of where you are. In the Wicklow mountains, where there is much gently shelving terrain the direction of slope might give a clue. Similarly, a stream's direction might be some use. It might be worthwhile to climb to the nearest top, identify it and start again if it would not be too tiring and demoralizing. If you can find one of the navigationally important landmarks noted in this book, it should be a great help.

If darkness is descending it is probably better to face a long road walk (you might get a lift) rather than take a 'short cut' across the hills. Don't plunge into a forestry plantation unless you are absolutely sure that you can emerge at the other side. You may make some progress at first and then find your way completely blocked by impenetrable closely spaced trees - and totally disoriented to cap it all.

WHAT TO CARRY WITH YOU

If you were to carry all the safety equipment that some experts tell you to carry, you would be so weighed down that you wouldn't be able to walk. The most important item to get right are boots, as mentioned above. Apart from that there are only a few things that you really must carry. These include food and a flask with a hot liquid, a whistle and a map and compass. Unless the day looks uncommonly settled and likely to remain so, you should take a waterproof. Lastly, you need a rucksack to put everything else in. Anything else is optional or depends mainly on the weather and the route.

A FEW ROUTE SELECTIONS

If you have limited time in Wicklow and want to get some idea of the flavour of the mountains as well as walking some of the best routes you might like to consider the following selection:

- Route 2, an area close to Dublin which avoids most of the degradation associated with the city's proximity;
- Route 6, an easy route in one of the loveliest areas in the mountains;
- Route 12, probably the most dramatic approach to Wicklow's highest peak;
- Route 18, a lovely circuit in Wicklow's favourite walking area;
- Route 28, Wicklow at its bleakest, yet a satisfying circuit.

PLANNING YOUR OWN ROUTES

The Wicklow mountains are the largest area of uplands in Ireland, much of it a wilderness but, by the standard of Irish mountains (note qualification!) without many dangerous areas. They therefore offer unrivalled scope for devising your own routes.

You will note from some of the route descriptions that information is given about the ease with which that particular route may be varied. In general it is easier to vary routes where there are no narrow ridges and cliffs, as is mostly the case in Wicklow, and where there has been little forestry planting, as is mostly *not* the case in Wicklow. Unless you know what you are doing it is advisable, if you want to walk anywhere near farmed areas, to start routes at points mentioned in this book; landowners are understandably sensitive about trespassers and the possible damage that uninvited 'guests' can cause.

THE COUNTRY CODE

It is surely not necessary to spell out the whole of the Country Code in detail, as it is just ordinary good manners adapted to the outdoors. Instead let's concentrate on a few of the possibly less obvious points.

- Car parking. On Sundays many mountain carparks are clogged with cars. Try to minimise over-crowding by sharing cars. Do not park along narrow roads, at driveways or gates or where your car will cause an obstruction to others;
- Dogs are a menace in the mountains, as they are in any sheep-rearing area. If you must take one, keep it on a lead for the entire walk;
- If you have to climb a closed gate do at the hinged end where you will cause less damage;
- Path erosion is an ever-increasing eyesore. Don't widen paths by walking on their edges. Either walk down their centre (despite the mud) or walk well away from the path altogether. Don't walk straight up or down hills if there is a zig-zag path. There are places in this book where I have avoided the 'obvious' path because it is eroded. Take especial care in soft, boggy country as it is particularly fragile;
- Don't climb fences unless there is simply no alternative. If you do, don't stand on the fence wires. They may look the same afterwards but will have been irretrievably damaged;
- Don't litter. Don't leave any, even biodegradable. Do you know how long it takes an orange peel to degrade? Think how unsightly it looks in the meantime. You might even consider taking away other people's litter. This might seem a pretty bizarre idea but it won't take much effort and litter cannot remove itself.

YOU, LANDOWNERS AND THE LAW

The only areas where the walker has right of way are on the Wicklow Way, in certain designated forest areas and in the National Park. Luckily for walkers the National Park now covers large areas in the uplands, probably a larger area than shown on the OS maps. However, in nearly all other areas the walker is there without the permission of the landowner, and therefore should leave if told to do so, unless of course there are serious safety implications.

The Occupiers' Liability Act 1995 has cleared up the matter of compensation if an accident occurs on a landowner's land. The walker is in the same legal category as a trespasser and the onus of responsibility for the walker's safety now rests on him/her - as of course it should - and not on the landowner, as the law may have been interpretable up to this. In theory at least this should make landowners a little more tolerant of walkers.

However you should try to avoid the following more difficult circumstances, any of which makes it more likely that you will clash with a local landowner:

- Being near homesteads or in enclosed fields, crossing fences, walls or gates;
- Walking in the lower hills near Dublin. Landowners in this area have suffered serious vandalism from yobbos and are understandably on short fuses;
- Being members of a large party (so they say anyway: if I were a landowner I would prefer a large 'ruly' party to a small unruly one);
- Having a dog, especially if unleashed;
- Generally behaving in an inconsiderate manner.

I have tried to steer you away from areas of conflict that I know about but it is impossible to forecast where trouble might flare in the future.

THEY'RE YOUR MOUNTAINS, TOO!

Ireland is a country with a 'healthy disregard' for the law, and no wonder, since the law in too many instances is only for show and not for enforcement. The end result of all this as far as the environment is concerned is littering, dumping, car wrecks, plastic from silage bales, all sorts of other agricultural waste, 'temporary dwellings' that moulder away for decades, and all the rest which are obvious to anyone who wants to see.

I wish there were a simple solution to all this, but there isn't. The best you can do is to obey the law yourself and join one of the voluntary organisations which care about the environment. If you are in a walking club, help its conservation group or suggest that one be formed if there isn't one.

ROUTE 1: KIPPURE AND THE UPPER LIFFEY VALLEY

Lots of boggy ground on a pleasant but far from spectacular route high on the broad ridge between Seefingan and Kippure, with good views in places. The walk ends with an easy stretch partly along the banks of the infant River Liffey.

Getting There Drive towards *Blessington,* turning left onto the R759 just past the village of Brittas. From this turn follow signs for Sally Gap for 5.7 miles, parking in the inconspicuous forest carpark on the left (GR 079144). It may be more convenient to come from the *Sally Gap* direction. In this case park on the rough ground on the left just after a prominent bridge (at GR 109127) 1.7 miles north-west of Sally Gap and start the walk from there.

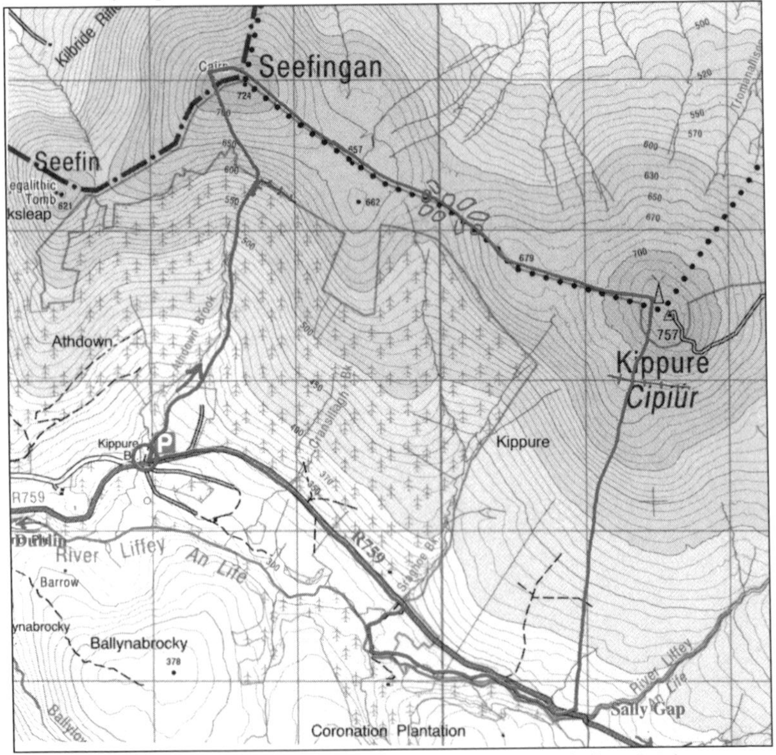

Walking Time 5 hours (distance 13km, climb 560m) including 0.5 hours over Naismith for difficult underfoot conditions.

Difficulties Fairly easy navigationally. If you get lost there is always the life-line of the R759 close at hand – but beware forest on the way. Otherwise only lots of bog to worry about.

Map Sheet 56.

Route From the carpark take the track for a few minutes and where it enticingly crosses the Athdown Brook on the left, do not follow it. Instead keep to the muddy track on the bank you are on and where it expires in forest, walk onward keeping the Brook within reach. Don't stick rigidly to it, because with difficult ground underfoot you may prefer to cross a fence close on the right, and walk upward over somewhat easier ground.

However you manage it you will shortly emerge onto an intermittent path, mature forest on the other side of the Brook, young forest on its near side. At length you will leave both Brook and forest behind, and shortly after, at a fence corner, one leg of which runs roughly east parallel to the Seefingan to Kippure ridge, take a bearing of about 340° compass for the great megalithic tomb just to the west of the top of Seefingan. (In bad conditions it might be prudent to simply walk north uphill to the crest of the ridge and set out for the tomb from there.)

From the tomb walk 200m east to the summit (a notional one) and then follow a ditch south-east along the county boundary. As it approaches a horrible area of peat hags set in an expanse of flat, black mud just to the south-east of pt 657m the ditch supinely disappears. You, however must carry on across this area heading for, and climbing summit 679m, where on easier ground the ditch re-appears. All along here the views, especially to the south are good, with Mullaghcleevaun particularly evident. However most of your attention will probably be headed downward as you navigate a way through the mud.

Summit 679m hasn't even a cairn. It does however provide a grandstand view of Kippure, whose near side is a swirl of peat hags and crevasses with a few improbable grassy stretches reaching towards the summit. So from summit 679m it is a simple matter to drop slightly into the col facing Kippure and then climb through one of these grassy stretches to the nearby summit.

Kippure (757m, 3 hours) is the highest point in county Dublin and commands fairly good views, though otherwise it hasn't a lot to recommend it, as it is a rounded summit whose few natural charms are negated by its burden of the TV mast, discarded artefacts and ancillary buildings.

From the summit head south at about 200° compass towards the R759, cross a sturdy but unbarbed fence on the way, and then descend into high heather. As you near the road, head towards the few scattered pines forming the eastern corner of the Coronation Plantation, cross it (the road) and turn right onto the rough path along a stream, the infant Liffey.

This is a nice, peaceful stretch: the river gurgling in its rocky bed and the old, dark pines of the Plantation standing out against the almost yellow grasses of the bogland. Walk downstream to a bridge over the river, serving a house set among the trees. Don't cross it: instead take the track up to the nearby road. Turn left here to walk the remaining 2km back to the start, an attractive walk through forest, scattered trees, moorland and even a little farmland.■

ROUTE 2: THE LOUGH BRAYS AND KIPPURE

It is possible to wring a good walk out of the wet and gently shelving moorland north of Kippure. The walk takes in the deep cleft of Mareen's Brook and the fine cliffs overlooking the large corrie lakes of the Lough Brays, thus proving that you can sometimes make a fairly decent silk purse out of a sow's ear.

Getting There Turn left into *Glenasmole*, keeping on the main road for about 2 miles to cross a prominent concrete bridge over a water channel debouching into the nearby reservoir. Set your milometer here. At 0.4 miles pass a minor road on the left. At about 0.7 miles look out suitable places to park along the road, taking care not to block entrances. The starting point indicated on the map is at the hairpin bend at the head of the road where there is space for only a few carefully parked cars (GR 109199). If you have a fleet of cars in your party see the variation below.

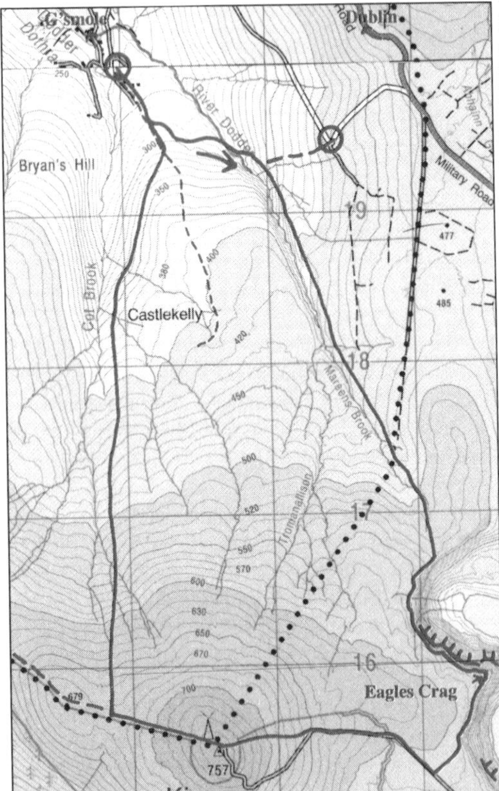

Walking Time 4.75 hours (distance 14km, climb 600m).

Difficulties Some wet ground underfoot and bracken which may be unpleasant in high summer. Navigation needs some attention but overall is not too demanding.

Map Sheet 56, though sheet 50 may also be useful in getting to the start, if you want to do the long variation or fear that you are going to go astray to the north of the route.

Route Let's say we are starting at the hairpin bend. Cross the gate here and take the track beyond, which winds upward into rough open country. After less than 10 minutes leave it and head south-east to the deep cleft of the Dodder, upstream to be renamed Mareen's Brook. A few hundred metres farther on you will be standing on the bank high above the stream and have two choices: you can continue along the bank or you can make a precipitous descent to walk along the stream. If you choose the latter you will be spared the panorama of millions of acres of bogland, of which there is a plentitude later in the walk.

This river walk is a surprisingly pleasant stretch: the deep-set stream plunging as an occasional low waterfall and, in its downstream reaches, mature broadleaf trees on the steeper western bank. Continue uphill and south-east along the Brook for about 3km, during which it gradually attains the general level of the bogland. There is only one major tributary along all this stretch, at which you take the eastern branch. Then, where it unravels close to its source, there intrudes an unwelcome sign of 'civilisation': the end of a bog road edged by rubbish, litter and dumping. A fine indication of our 'care' for the environment. Here, press on south-east across featureless bog to reach the edge of the cliffs overlooking Lower Lough Bray only a few hundred metres away.

The first sight of Lough Bray is quite dramatic: its broad and usually tranquil waters, the solitary house set among trees on its shore and above all (both senses) the steep cliffs curving round to Eagle's Crag.

The idea now is to turn right to follow the wide path at the edge of the cliffs to and beyond Eagle's Crag, passing on the way a deep cleft where a stream has eaten into the cliff edge. Eagle's Crag overlooks both the Lough Brays so it is worthwhile making the slight detour to take in the view. I find the Upper Lake a bit disappointing after the Lower. Maybe it lacks its variety and dramatic setting.

From Eagle's Crag keep on the path high above the Upper Lake for about another 10 minutes and then head south-west across moorland to reach the nearby TV road. From here it is an easy slog up to the summit of Kippure (757m, 3.25 hours). You need not take the road all the way - near the TV mast you can climb directly to the summit. Of Kippure, least said, soonest mended, though in its favour it might be noted that the views are extensive.

The rest of the walk is easy to describe. Though not strictly necessary, you will be sure of reaching the headwaters of the Cot Brook by walking west to the nearby col facing summit 679m and at its boggy bottom heading north. Keep the main stream somewhere on the left as you descend (the exact route is immaterial), crossing minor tributaries as you do so.

As you approach the woods, fields and houses of upper Glenasmole you will have to swing right away from the Brook to reach the track on which you started. As you can see from the modified map given here this track extends much further south than shown on sheet 56. It offers an easy route if the vegetation near the river becomes too trying. Turn left downhill onto it to reach the start.

Longer Variation From Kippure you may be tempted to walk to Seefingan and Corrig, but I trust, only if you have sheet 50 (see also route 3). From Corrig walk north-east to pick up a track running north-west and ending at a minor road at GR 098208. Walking time is 6.25 hours (distance 19km, climb 820m).

Alternative Start If you have more than several cars in your party drive the *Military Road* past Killakee carpark (GR 122223). Take the second turn right beyond it to park a short distance down at about a sharp corner (GR 124194) around which there are places to park on the roadside. Start the route by walking south-west a few hundred metres to the Dodder/Mareen's Brook. ■

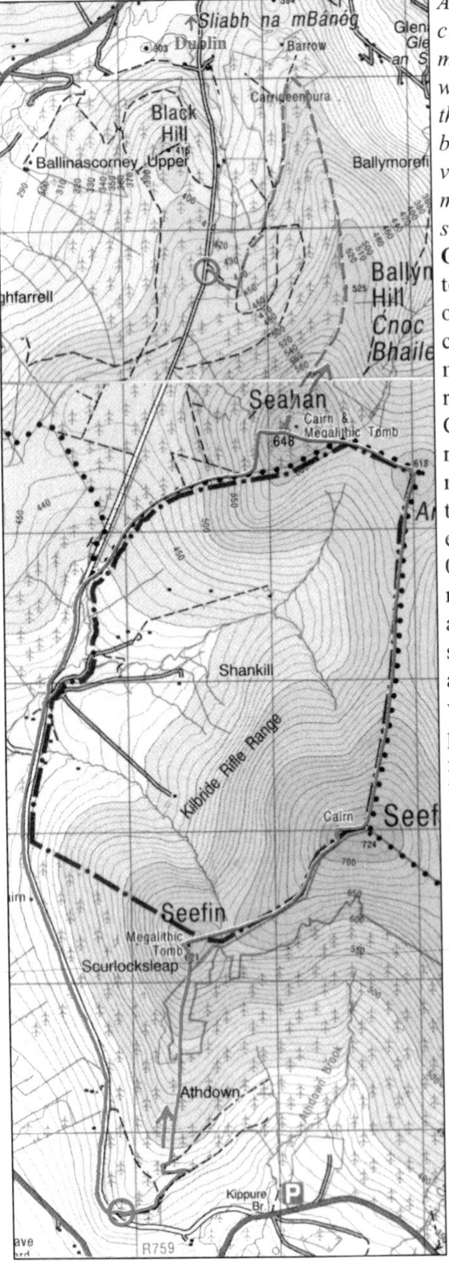

A short walk in the north-west corner of the range, across mountains which are gently sloped, with many areas of forestry on their lower reaches and much soft bogland higher up. However the views are extensive and the megalithic tombs on three of the summits add a touch of the exotic.

Getting There Take the R114 towards *Glenasmole* but instead of turning left into the valley, continue straight ahead for 0.4 miles to fork left onto a minor road (set your milometer here). Continue straight ahead on a narrow potholed road for 5.1 miles and park in the second of two closely spaced forest entrances on the left (GR 068144). Alternatively you can reach this point from the R759 on a longer but better road. You will see from the map that you can also park anywhere along the road within 2.7 miles north of the proposed starting point and face a road walk first rather than last.

Walking Time 4.5 hours (distance 14km, climb 600m).

Difficulties Much soggy ground. Navigation is moderately easy but in bad visibility the gently sloping moorland with few definite features can be intimidating.

Map Sheet 56.

Route Take the track heading east (right) from the forest entrance, keeping to the main one where a minor track branches right at a hairpin bend. Continue round one right-angle bend (to the right) and at a second, turn left uphill on a clear path and firebreak, immediately crossing another track.

Now out of the trees, at least to the extent that you can see over them, views expand to include Pollaphuca Reservoir and the foothills of the mountains to the south-west. Continue upward on what is eventually a muddy firebreak to emerge onto the heathery higher slopes of Seefin (621m) and walk to the modest summit, crowned by a far from modest megalithic tomb (1).

From Seefin drop to a nearby shallow col to the east and then resume the gentle but continuous climb through heather, accompanied for part of the way by old fence posts on the right. These however veer away across the slope within about 10 minutes of the summit - or rather of the huge megalithic tomb on Seefingan (724m).

In bad visibility it is important to realize that this tomb does not mark the summit: this feeble and indistinct rise in the general level of the bogland lies about 200m further east. From here, and not from the tomb, you are square with the broad ridge leading to Corrig to the north, reached on an eroded path along the county boundary and more to the point, also the boundary of a rifle range, so don't wander west. Corrig (618m), an unassuming peak, hasn't a megalithic tomb and has to make do with a modest WD marker. From here head directly to Seahan (648m, 2.75 hours), which in addition to a trig pillar has the third megalithic tomb of the day, an insignificant looking grassy affair. In spite of indications to the contrary on sheet 56, there are no trees on the summit of Seahan, though a forestry plantation, the next target, is only a few minutes away.

Head roughly west from the summit and at the plantation turn left to follow its edge. This will take you for a few paces south, but shortly the edge swings west, so that you are walking down a wide firebreak, chivvied by Army warning notices on the left (you are again on the edge of the rifle range). You can follow the forest, and later also a stream all the way down to the road, where you turn left to face a walk of over 4km on tarmac back to the car. Initially it is possible to walk parallel to the road in upland fields rather than walk tarmac, but sooner rather than later you will be forced onto the road. This is a gentle walk between forest and fields, marred only by litter, your inevitable companion on most Irish roads.

Two Car Variation With a second car you can make a longer walk northwards along the crest of the high ground. You will need sheet 50 as well as sheet 56.

Leave one car at a forest entrance on the left 1.3 miles from the point where you turned off the R114 (GR 076207). Take the main route to the summit of Seahan from where a compass bearing of about 20° will get you to a forest corner and onto sheet 50. Continue roughly north along its edge until you enter dense trees on a rough and muddy path. This ends shortly on a track, where you turn left, and left again at the nearby junction. Walk straight ahead for about 1.5km, then turn right to reach the car, which should be visible from here. Walking time is 4.25 hours (distance 13km, climb 620m).

Note

(1) Megalithic Tombs: More properly called passage graves, they date from about 2000 BC, and consist of mounds of stones with a burial chamber at the centre, entered by a long narrow passage. They are often found in groups and on summits, like those encountered on this route. ■

ROUTE 4: ROCKBROOK, TWO ROCK TO ENNISKERRY

Starting from the outskirts of Dublin this linear route traverses the eastern fringe of the hills and encompasses a wide variety of terrain – wood, moorland and hillside. Given its location, the route has no real feeling of remoteness but, in spite of neglect and litter, is as attractive as you are likely to get close to the city.

Getting There Take the 47A bus to Rockbrook (note times as the service is infrequent). Alternatively you could take the 47 bus (also infrequent) but this involves an extra walk: turn left into Cloragh Road to get onto the route proper. At the end take the 44 bus from Enniskerry; it runs about every hour. Note the alternative starts below.

Walking Time 6.5 hours (distance 20km, climb 750m).

Difficulties A few places where attention to navigation might be advisable. Some wet ground but generally fairly firm underfoot.

Map Both sheets 50 and 56. Their depiction of tracks is as usual poor.

Route Let's say you are in Rockbrook village (GR 1324). What follows are tedious directions, but I fear there is little alternative.

Anyway off we go. From the village take the Tibradden Road steeply downhill, continue straight ahead on Mutton Lane where it shortly swings left and turn right to keep on Mutton Lane rather than taking the cul de sac road ahead. After about a kilometre steadily uphill, and here you are into farming land on the lower slopes of the hills, take a barred forest track on the right. That's the end of tarmac for a while, but not of boring directions. However if you really cannot be bothered with them keep walking upward and south-east until you are on the crest of the Tibradden spur, with a tor (heap of granite rocks) on your right. Pick up the commentary in the paragraph after next.

Otherwise: walk the forest track to fork first left uphill and then turn first left onto a rising path. After a few paces take a narrow path on the right through dense trees, cross a track and continue uphill to a tee. Turn left here. At last you are out of forest on a rising track heading along the crest of the Tibradden spur. Fork right shortly and you will come to the tor mentioned above. Complicated directions over – for a while.

You are now on a level stretch with fairly good views south over Cruagh Mountain across upper Glencullen. Keep to the deteriorating track until you reach a tee and the Wicklow Way. Turn left uphill here and, still with the Way, turn sharply right thus heading for the cairn and trig pillar on the top of Fairy Castle (536m). Where the Way swings left keep straight ahead to reach the nearby summit.

Fairy Castle gives good views over much of the north-east of the range and a long stretch of coast, though it's admittedly not the most impressive part of either range or coast. From it walk south-east on a clear path for 200m or so to Two Rock, crowned by an outcrop (the tors which give the mountain its name lie over a fence just beyond it). From Two Rock a compass bearing of about 210° might be useful, the idea being to reach the R116, which runs through Glencullen, at GR 170209. Because of gorse along the line of the bearing you will not be able to keep on it for long, but it's better than nothing. As you approach the road look out for, and walk between, two parallel fences about two metres apart and heading directly for it. If you miss them completely try to reach the road to the west rather than the east, as there are more houses eastward.

Once on the road turn left (you are now back on the Way) and take the first turn right, thus crossing the Glencullen River at Boranaraltry Bridge. Follow the Way south-east, admiring as you go the rough fields surrounded by sturdy stone walls down on the left. At this point you cross over onto sheet 56 and just onto it turn

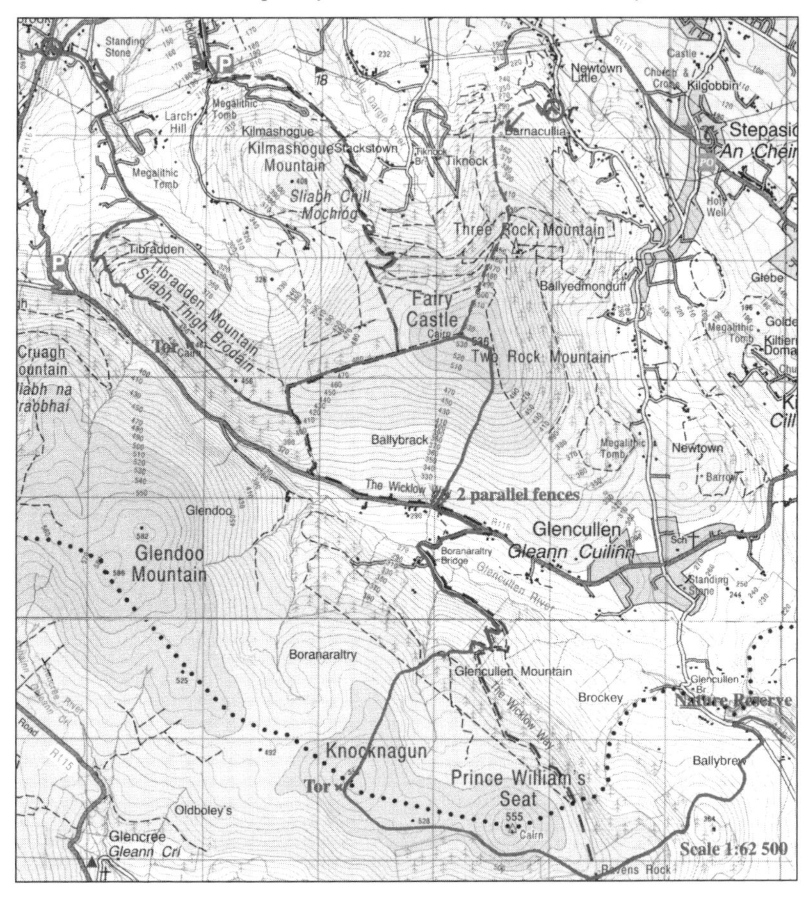

right with the Way (I found the waymark ambiguous). Still on a track climb through felled trees onto the shoulder of Knocknagun. Higher up you will come to a tee, onto which you turn right to leave the Way. Follow this track for a short distance until it passes over a bridge and here take a rough path on the left to reach open country with Knocknagun, the next target, to the south-west. Say farewell to tracks and paths for a while and prepare for a walk through high grass and heather.

You cannot mistake Knocknagun (555m, 4.25 hours) since it is topped by a formidable tor on its southern side, a good substitute for a proper summit, which it doesn't possess. There is an all too obvious eroded path to nearby Prince William's Seat to the east so please do not use it. Instead keep the crest of the broad ridge on the left and head roughly south-east to the corner of forest, a route that gives good views over Glencree and in particular towards the cliffs of the Raven's Glen to the south. When you near the forest keep it somewhere below on the right, aiming to reach it at its far corner.

At this corner you will pick up the Wicklow Way again; it enters forest, but you don't. Instead head east along a narrow path through heather to the two outcrops close by which constitute Ravens Rock. From these outcrops continue on a path running north-east and gradually converging with mature forest on the right. Where the path crosses a track you will have to look out carefully for its extension on the other side; it's in thick forest a few metres to the left of a stone wall and initially requires some faith to identify.

Take it to where the slope levels out in a clearing you will encounter a track on the right making a sharp turn. Turn left onto it to shortly reach another sharp turn. Turn left off the track here to cross an undependable stile and so emerge from forest onto a rough field. This point marks the last of the long distance views so this might be a good opportunity to view the coast and the few minor hills facing it. Then you can set off directly downhill to reach a track onto which you turn left and right at the nearby junction (we're back into tedious directions territory).

Once on tarmac turn left. Walk for only a few hundred metres downhill and then look out for a stile on the right leading into forest. Curiously this stile is superfluous to requirements, as you can easily reach a narrow path running into thick forest without it.

You are now in Knocksink Nature Reserve and on the path which will take you nearly all the way into Enniskerry about 3km away. It is a lovely wood, mainly coniferous here at the top and completely deciduous further down. The path runs sometimes high above a deep ravine, sometimes close to the surging Glencullen River at its bottom. It is easy enough to follow though it does make a few perilous swoops. Remember to keep to the path even though at one or two points an alternative route into fields looks far more attractive. When you reach the road in Enniskerry turn right to reach the village centre and the bus.

Alternative Starts You can start at Marley Park (GR 1526) with bus routes 14, 14A, 16, 47B or 48A within range. Take the Wicklow Way to near the summit of Fairy Castle and follow the commentary from there.

You can also start in Barnacullia (GR 1824) on the east of the range (bus route 44B). From the Blue Light pub walk north, take the first turn on the left, walk past the quarry into rough ground on the northern slopes of Three Rock. Walk roughly south-west to forest, then take the path to the summit (a pincushion of masts). Walk south from there to Fairy Castle. ■

ROUTE 5: FANCY AND KNOCKNACLOGHOGE

One of the best routes in the Wicklow mountains: a lovely interplay of rugged mountain and cliff, wooded valleys and large, beautifully located lakes.

Getting There By car drive towards *Glendalough*, turning right off the R755 onto the R759 about 7 miles south of Kilmacanoge. Drive 2 miles to park near the prominent gate pillars on the left ('Pier Gates') (GR 173064), *not* the much smaller gate pillars just before them. If you are travelling by St Kevin's bus take it to the junction of the R755 and the R759 (GR 2005) and walk from there (3km each way).

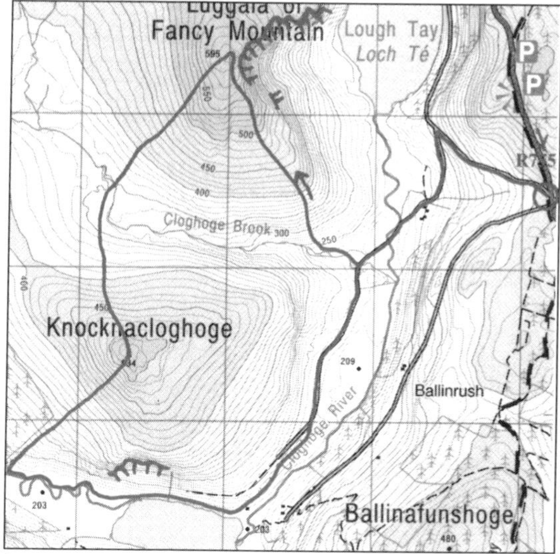

Walking Time 4.5 hours (distance 13km, climb 780m).

Difficulties One stream to be forded. Otherwise easy.

Map Sheet 56.

Route From Pier Gates, you can see practically the entire route: the cliffs of Luggala topped by Fancy, bumpy Knocknacloghoge leftward, at whose foot and just out of sight lies Lough Dan. An inviting prospect!

Walk the tarmacadam road at the Gates (at one point on the descent you will see a path offering a short-cut, a welcome alternative to tarmac). On the valley floor and now on a track, cross one bridge and immediately turn right to follow another track westward. Leave it shortly to climb directly to the summit of Fancy (595m), a tough climb with widening views, best as you near the summit where cliffs close on the right plunge directly in rocky precipices and boulders into Lough Tay.

Fancy's summit is a letdown: a mundane, grassy plateau. Never mind, the long views are no disappointment. From Fancy head south-west over heather towards Knocknacloghoge. Do not go directly south as this would give a difficult crossing over the Cloghoge Brook: it's difficult enough as it is. Once across it head to the summit of Knocknacloghoge (534m), a fine, rocky point giving excellent views of Lough Dan and much more besides. Walk south-west from the summit to follow a forestry fence and so reach the Inchavore River at the Copse, a group of deciduous trees on the opposite bank.

Walk east from here following the river downstream to pass through a wet area below cliffs flanking the southern side of Knocknacloghoge. Here a delightful path materialises along the shore of Lough Dan. Walk it to a two-storey house close to the Cloghoge River, where it improves to a track, then continue along the valley floor, all the way in splendid country, to finally face the steep uphill to Pier Gates. There had to be retribution for the initial easy downhill! ■

ROUTE 6: MAULIN AND THE TONDUFFS

To start, a forest track that gives good views to and over Glencree, followed by difficult ground underfoot to reach shelving bogland. After Tonduff South, sharper, more defined terrain and improving views open up to Maulin and beyond.

Getting There Drive to *Enniskerry*, here follow signs for Glendalough for 2 miles, then turn right off the main road at a tee. Pass the prominent gates of Powerscourt on the left and park in the large Crone carpark after another mile (GR 192142). This point may also be reached from the Military Road by turning off it at the sign 'Glencree Drive'.

Walking Time 4.5 hours (distance 14km, climb 620m).

Difficulties Although the distance under high vegetation to be walked is not long it may be quite exhausting. It is therefore advisable not to attempt this walk in high summer and autumn when the bracken is at its worst. Navigation is difficult after leaving the initial forest tracks but you can minimise problems by heading directly for Tonduff South, rather than climbing Powerscourt Mountain.

Map Sheet 56.

Route From the end of the carpark take the one and only track through mature forest and, ignoring a fork left after a few metres, keep on it heading roughly west for about 1km to reach an open area with the stern and impressive slabs and crags of the Raven's Glen high up on the left.

Continue on the track into more mature forest, ignoring grassy minor tracks. At the one doubtful junction, fork right rather than left uphill. Shortly after this you will cross a considerable stream and beyond it come to another junction, with a track downhill to the right, a narrow grassy track on the level straight ahead and a track heading uphill on the left, the one you want. Shortly after you will get your first glimpse of the northern end of the spur that is Powerscourt Mountain, your first goal. Pass two tracks on the left and where your track swings decisively left (south-east) you will have an opportunity to consider the climb to Powerscourt Mountain, reached by first crossing rough ground and a stream. The stream is maybe 100m away, but to get there you will have to struggle through high heather – good practice for what lies ahead.

Once at it walk upstream diverting right away from it anywhere, perhaps at about a few isolated trees. Then climb roughly west through high heather and bracken to reach the crest of the spur, a tough ascent. Once on the crest you will be compensated by views of Eagles Crag, the corrie of Upper Lough Bray and the mast on Kippure, the latter not a thing of beauty but at least useful as an identifiable feature. Keep on the crest to skirt round the upper valley of the stream you were alongside and then climb to Tonduff South (about 640m, 3 hours), which has a boulder on its summit beside which are what looks like purposeful markings on two granite slabs – remnants of a sculpture sited in this unlikely location.

From the summit walk east to cross boggy ground and pass pt 593m, a mound that you are unlikely to notice. Then continue along the southern side of the Raven's Glen, now on an eroded path giving good views down into the Glen as well as over Glencree, and so reach firmer, steeper ground and a few rocky steps on the way to Maulin's summit, the only distinct one on this route.

Maulin (570m) gives good views over the mountains, with Djouce prominent to the south and, in clear visibility even the corrie holding Cleevaun Lough far off to the south-west. In addition, because of its location at the edge of the range, it also gives good views seaward, all along the coast from Howth to Wicklow Head and perhaps beyond.

Having assimilated all this continue east, still on an eroded path, but here edged by high heather, for about a kilometre, until you come to a partly tumbled wall

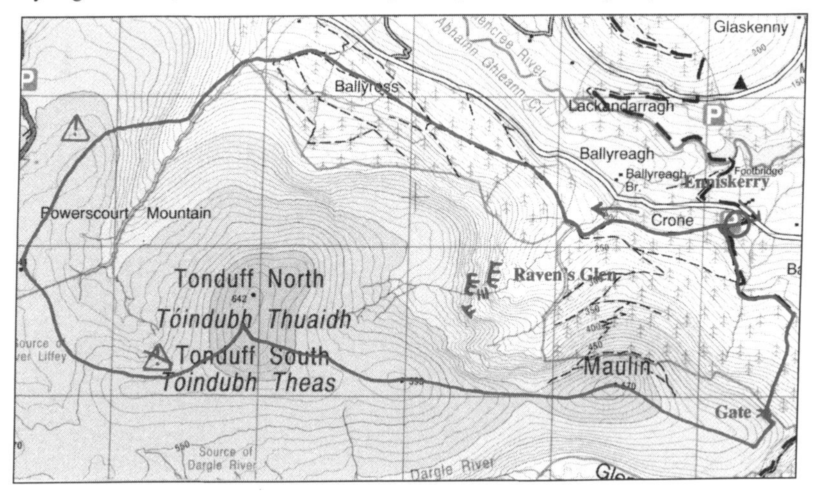

with a rough path running alongside it. Turn left downhill here for a short distance, until you come close to thick forest ahead, with a wall running west just before it.

Time to head for home. Keeping the forest close on the right walk for about 100m from the wall junction to a sturdy gate at the entrance to the forest. Cross it and it will take you directly downhill through the forest, across a forest track and down to the main forest track, directly beyond which are upland fields. Turn left here and walk to a Wicklow Way marker at a junction. Turn right at it and sharply first right again to reach the carpark. ■

ROUTE 7: MULLAGHCLEEVAUN EAST TOP AND LOUGH DAN

Quite a contrast between a walk along the gently sloping, high but fairly dull hills forming the spine of the range and a lengthy but scenic stroll beside streams flowing into Lough Dan. The route can be easily split into two shorter routes.

Getting There By car to *Sally Gap*. Continue south (that is towards Glendalough) to park 4.1 miles farther on just before the road enters forestry (GR 113073). There is space to park several cars off the road here and a few places to park more cars a little farther on. Don't park even partly on the road.

Walking Time 6 hours (distance 17km, climb 720m), including about a quarter hour over Naismith for difficult underfoot conditions along the Inchavore River.

Difficulties Because of the lack of features in the first half of the route navigation may be difficult in bad weather but there are no dangerous areas anywhere around; you can always head for the Military Road. High vegetation is the problem in the second half, so it is best to avoid this section in high summer.

Map Sheet 56.

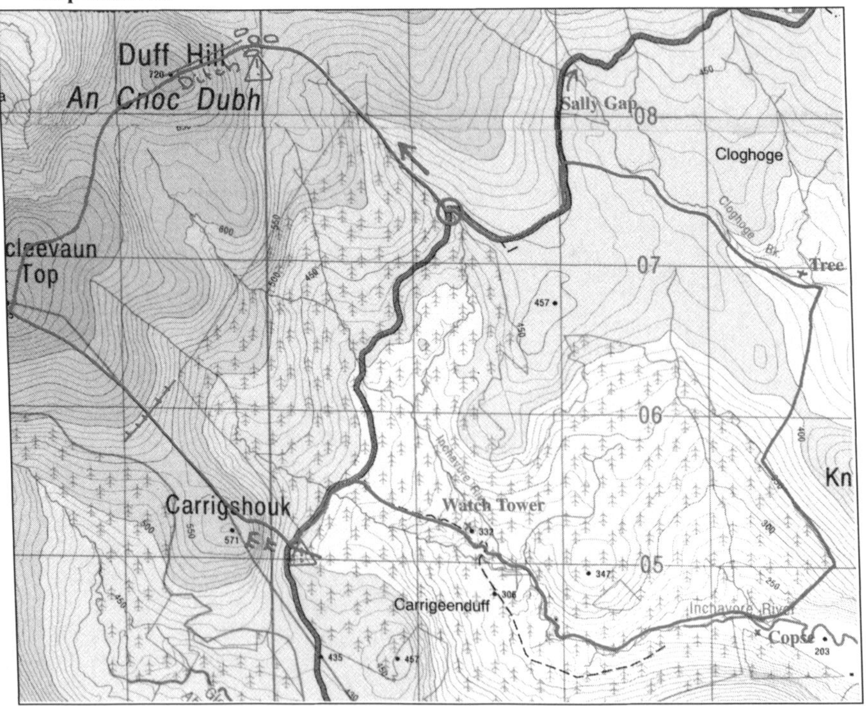

Route Walk north-west following a stream and forestry on the left to the far end of the plantation and from there continue north-west to the col between Gravale on the right and Duff Hill on the left. At this point, as well as encountering peat hags in a wet area, you will also meet a wide, intermittent ditch heading south-west to north-east, which, although not evident here at the col is a useful navigational feature higher up.

The summit of Duff Hill (720m) is the next target. Duff is one of a line of hills along the spine of the range which have no great pretensions to individuality, though it does have a modest boulder field on its summit. From it the route continues south-west to Mullaghcleevaun East Top, where you should be a little careful, especially in bad visibility. This is because the East Top has, in fact, two tops, with the lower one (about 770m) climbed first. From it walk south about 400m to the East Top itself (795m). From here you may be tempted to climb Mullaghcleevaun, the rim of whose northern corrie is not much more than a kilometre away; it is a much more impressive mountain than any climbed so far. A there-and-back should take about 40 minutes.

From the East Top descend south-east along a broad spur passing a fence on the way to Carrigshouk (571m). Not to the summit of Carrigshouk, because on its far side are short but wicked slabs. Instead gradually descend on a narrow path along the flank of Carrigshouk keeping higher ground on the right. This will lead you, via a few gates and fences, back to the road, the Military Road of course (2.75 hours). Turn left onto it to reach a forest track on the right a few hundred metres away. Here you can cut the route short by walking over 2km onward along the road to the start.

Let's assume you want to keep going. Turn onto the track and when you pass a watch tower after about 10 minutes, look out for some gouged out ground on the left a few minutes later. Turn left (east) here to find and walk a rough track for a few metres through trees to a shaky bridge over the Inchavore River. Cross it to reach an intermittent path on the far bank.

Walk downstream for about 3km to a copse of deciduous trees on the far bank and a stile on the near one. There are several options from here: you can climb Knocknacloghoge and pick up the main route again at the Cloghoge Brook to its north; you can continue downstream to walk the shores of Lough Dan and the Cloghoge River and Brook (a highly scenic but long variation - see also route 5) or you can climb to the col north-west of Knocknacloghoge, the main route.

For the latter follow a forestry fence uphill north-east and then north-west. After about a kilometre on the latter tack head north-east to cross the col, all the while with gradually expanding views. Then descend about north-east to the Cloghoge Brook, set in a broad remote valley with fine hills to the east.

Walk upstream on the near bank and you will come close to a mountain ash, the only tree for miles around and so a good reassurance feature. Keep it on the right and you will take the correct tributary at the one point where there may be doubt. Follow this tributary into open moorland and when you see the Military Road ahead, or more likely the occasional car on that road, veer left away from the stream to trudge across bleak moorland and so reach it. Turn left on it to reach the nearby start.

ROUTE 8: SCARR FROM OLDBRIDGE

Scarr (641m) is one of the most shapely mountains in Wicklow, its summit a grassy, hummocky ridge offering excellent views. The trouble is that it stands a little aloof from the main chain and apart from combining it with Tonelagee it is a little difficult to make a long enough walk on its own. This short walk is probably most suitable for short winter days.

Getting There Drive to *Roundwood*. Turn right here following the signs for Lough Dan. Turn right at Oldbridge after $2^1/_2$ miles, still following these signs to park almost immediately on waste ground on the left (GR 158018).

Walking Time 4.5 hours (distance 14km, climb 540m).

Difficulties None.

Map Sheet 56 or the Glendalough Glenmalur 1:25 000 map.

Route Walk onward along the road, which gives lovely glimpses over Lough Dan. After about 15 minutes steady walking the road swings left over a bridge and degenerates to a track. A few metres up from the bridge cross a narrow gate on the right and follow the path beyond initially between high fences. This path gives enhanced views to Lough Dan and the long valley of the Cloghoge River to the north with Knocknacloghoge to its left.

All very easy so far, but now a little suffering. The path ends at a track, where you can opt for the minor variation (see below). Otherwise cross it and start climbing directly upward on a rough path through gorse to reach a mighty rock fronting a convenient stile. And with that short period of purgatory over, easy walking along the crest of a broad heathery spur begins. Along here by the way you might note Scarr, now off to the south-west, with its lower north-western top to its right.

This is the eastern and duller end of Kanturk Mountain, which isn't really a mountain, merely a long curving spur of upland. Keep to the crest of the spur to reach the more interesting western end, a fascinating rocky, hummocky area and well worth exploring. On your meanderings you should encounter a large egg-shaped rock, maybe 3m high, nearer the eastern end of the hummocky section, a modest landmark in bad visibility.

If you keep to the crest of the Kanturk spur you will be walking south-west at the end of the rocky ground. Here you should meet a path heading towards south towards Scarr via its north-west top, itself preceded by a navigationally reassuring standing stone. All along here the views are of course excellent with lofty Tonelagee dominating the western skyline.

You will reach an earthbank just before the summit of Scarr, but rather than take the ugly eroded path that climbs directly to the northern top, I suggest you veer left from it to cross low vegetation and so reach this top from Scarrr's north-east spur.

Scarr (641m, 2.75 hours) is one of the most individual of Wicklow's mountains, a long grassy summit with several tops, throwing out rounded spurs to the east where there is much wooded and agricultural country and commanding excellent views to the west where Tonelagee still dominates.

Now for the descent. Walk south along the line of grassy tops and then keep to the crest of the high ground to cross the same earthbank met on the climb (it circles the summit). After this you might start to keep an eye out for a forest corner well over a kilometre away to the south-east. It's easy to find: simply keep to the high ground running south and farther on south-east to pick up a narrow track near this corner. If you want further reassurance you might note that there is a gate near it, a rare object in these parts.

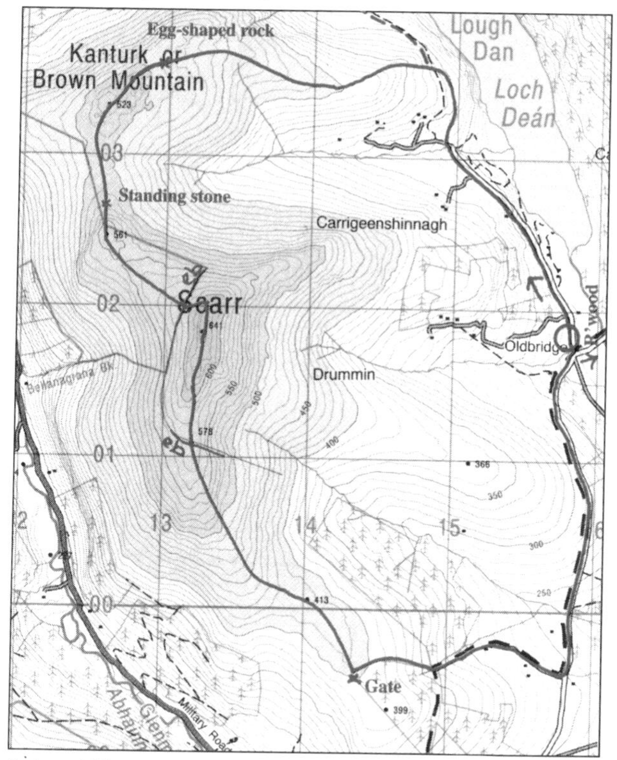

Turn left downhill at the corner keeping to what is probably a firebreak rather than a track. Here you have good views not only over the agricultural land ahead but also towards Scarr's spurs to the north. A short distance down it joins the Wicklow Way, here making a right-angle bend. Cross a stile to walk the east-running branch, which ends on the road (also part of the Way).

Turn left here to take it down dale, up hill and down dale again to reach Oldbridge about 2km away. Turn left here (hope you realized this already!) to reach the nearby parking place.

Minor Variation If you haven't already done so on another route you might like to continue on the track and so eventually walk parallel to the Inchavore River as far as the copse about a kilometre west of Lough Dan. Just beyond it take a firebreak directly uphill through dense trees to Kanturk. This variation gives lovely close views of the Inchavore River and the cliffs of Knocknacloghoge across the river. ■

ROUTE 9: FANCY AND DJOUCE

Excellent views over much of the route, with especially good, varied angles on Lough Tay snuggled below the great cliffs of Luggala. The centre section has some difficult vegetation underfoot and rather too much moorland.

Getting There Head towards *Glendalough*, turning right at Kilmacanoge onto the R755, and turn right again after 7 miles onto the R759. Continue uphill for 2.7 miles, parking in the second of two closely spaced carparks on the right (GR 169074). This point may also be easily reached from *Sally Gap.*

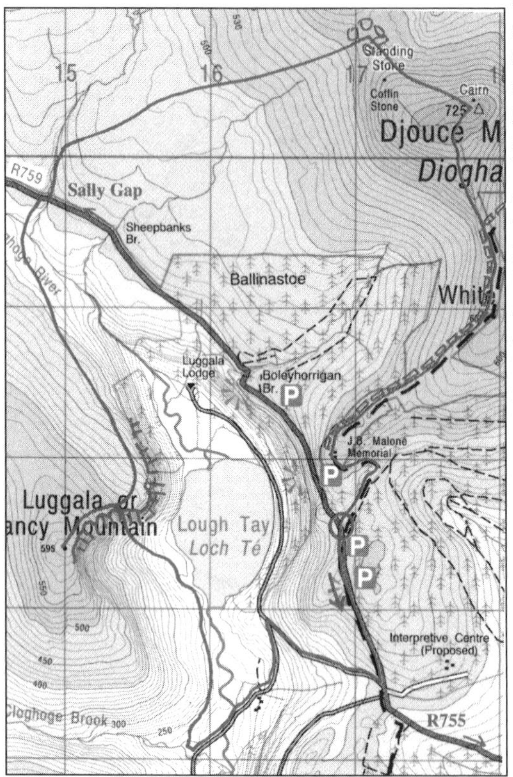

Walking Time 5.25 hours (distance 16km, climb 760m).

Difficulties As well as being rough underfoot as already mentioned, the centre section around the R759 requires attention to navigation.

Map Sheet 56

Route From the carpark walk south along the road, a stroll enlivened by the sight of Lough Tay tucked in down on the right below the cliffs of Fancy. There will be plenty of other lovely views of Lough Tay before the end of the walk.

After 1km turn right at a set of high pillars ('Pier Gates') to face – at a distance – the mighty cliffs terminating the eastern side of Fancy. Walk the road beyond the pillars to reach the floor of the valley (you may like to take a short cut on a rough path some distance down). On the valley floor and now in the midst of some of the most delectable scenery in Wicklow, cross one bridge, turn right onto a side track, cross a mighty stile and make a decision.

You can climb directly from here to the summit of Fancy (route 6) or you can take the adventurous option, the latter only if you do not suffer from severe vertigo and if visibility is good. For this option walk north from the stile following the Cloghoge Brook and when you come to the southern end of Lough Tay you will see a great sweep of cliff overlooking the lake. To its left, and north-west of where you are now, you will see steep ground with, way above it a mighty crag, leaving two obvious grassy gullies reaching to the summit of Fancy, one on each side of the crag. If you are not quite sure of what I mean do not attempt this!

You can climb by either side of the crag, the left gully later giving a longer walk along the cliff edge and therefore preferable. It's a straightforward climb, though over boulders and high vegetation lower down. When you reach the top of the cliffs, as on the climb up, the views are stupendous, particularly to Lough Tay with the great cliffs and boulders reaching down to it.

If you have taken the adventurous option it is probably worthwhile walking as far as the summit (595m) and then retracing steps. Then keep the cliffs on the right on a path that gradually becomes intermittent. To help you keep on it, it might be some help to say that it runs roughly above the scattered trees spreading up from the valley floor. As you approach the R759 again you will see the next target, the prominent bridge at GR 148096, reached by walking the bank of the Cloghoge River and then fording one of its branches. Around here there are, incidentally, excellent sheltered places to stop for a break.

At 2.75 hours into the walk and with the car only 3km away by road (hope you aren't tempted), cross the road and continue up the narrow, pleasant river valley beyond, then veer east away from it to cross wet moorland and so reach the haggy col between War Hill and Djouce.

Rather than follow the normal, eroded route south and east from the col to Djouce, I suggest you take a direct bearing so as to minimise damage. This will take you over rough ground but the time difference and views are pretty similar. Djouce (725m) is easy to recognise even in bad weather: as well as the trig pillar there are fangs of schist protruding from the summit grass.

From Djouce the rest is easy, both physically and navigationally and in addition offers lovely views, especially to the west towards the high peaks of Mullaghcleevaun and Tonelagee. Walk south-west from the summit for 100m or so and then swing south down the southern shoulder of Djouce. After less than 1km you will pick up the boardwalks of the Wicklow Way. Since the Way is to be followed to the end, navigational problems are behind – unless the route of the Way is altered.

With this possibility in mind a few directions are prudent. Follow the Way over hummocky terrain at White Hill and down past the JB Malone memorial, around which the boardwalks finish and from where there are renewed splendid vistas of Lough Tay. Turn left at forest and briefly enter it. Turn right at a nearby cross tracks to reach the nearby carpark. ■

ROUTE 10: DJOUCE AND WAR HILL

After a fairly dull start, a varied and easy walk with lovely, wide views from the southern spur of Djouce. It is followed by a stroll along the banks of Dargle River in the heart of narrow Glensoulan. Perhaps a bit short for summer but ideal for winter days.

Getting There Drive to *Enniskerry*, follow the signs for Glendalough in the village, turn right off the main road (signed 'Roundwood') after 2 miles, drive for a further 2.5 miles to park in the third of Djouce Woods carparks (GR 210107). This carpark is a little further south than shown on sheet 56.

Walking Time 4.25 hours (distance 13km, climb 550m).

Difficulties Some wet and eroded ground; easy navigationally.

Map Sheet 56.

Route Take the path from the carpark, cross a stream and climb westward into forest, crossing a fence on the left after a few hundred metres from the stream to reach open country east of Djouce. Keeping forest on the right ascend gently north-westwards to the crest of the hill, where you will meet a Wicklow Way waymark. Turn left here onto the Way.

It hasn't been very exciting so far. But now on the eastern shoulder of Djouce and with views opening up particularly over the plateau of Calary, prospects start to improve. Keep on the Wicklow Way, forking left with it where a horrible path has been gouged directly to the summit (please don't take it). The Way continues first on the level and then uphill to reach the crest of the long spur running south from Djouce.

From here to Djouce is a glorious stretch, with a wide panorama of peaks crowding the south and west horizons. The whole of this section is marked by a path, so the thing to remember is to swing right on the summit plateau. Djouce's summit (725m) is marked by a trig pillar and several fangs of rock rearing skyward. The views, encompassing a wide range of mountain and the coastal plain north and south of Dublin, are excellent.

The usual dogleg route along the crest from Djouce to War Hill is badly eroded in parts. To avoid at least some of it and slow down its degradation, head directly from the summit to close to the col south of War Hill (but not exactly to the col itself – it is dreadfully eroded). Unfortunately this means that you have a somewhat harder progress through high heather. You also miss the shelter of the well-named Coffin Stone for shelter and a food break. At least you can console yourself that you are on the high moral ground.

Climb directly from the col to the summit, marked by a modest few stones on an area of undistinguished bog. From here you can aim anywhere from north to north-east, the object being to reach the Dargle River in Glensoulan. On the way down you should be able to spot the remains of Grouse House (1) away to the west on pt 570m, a stark chimney stack in a stark landscape. Turn right downstream when you reach the river, and follow the bank along the narrow steep-sided valley, its austerity softened by the occasional ancient tree clinging to its slopes. A delightful stretch.

When you reach a forestry plantation, turn right steeply uphill to follow the forest edge on the left. Look out for a significant unplanted indentation in the forest about 15 minutes walk from the river. Turn left here to walk diagonally across the indentation, where you should pick up a path that heads roughly east into forest and shortly improves to a track.

Follow this track straight ahead through forest and after a few zig-zags, take a path on the right running steeply downhill, to reach the same track after it has executed a U turn. Continue on this track across the low ground left by the deceased Paddock Pond (2). Turn right at the far side of the low ground to walk along its length. At its southern end, with private property ahead turn left uphill to reach the carpark.

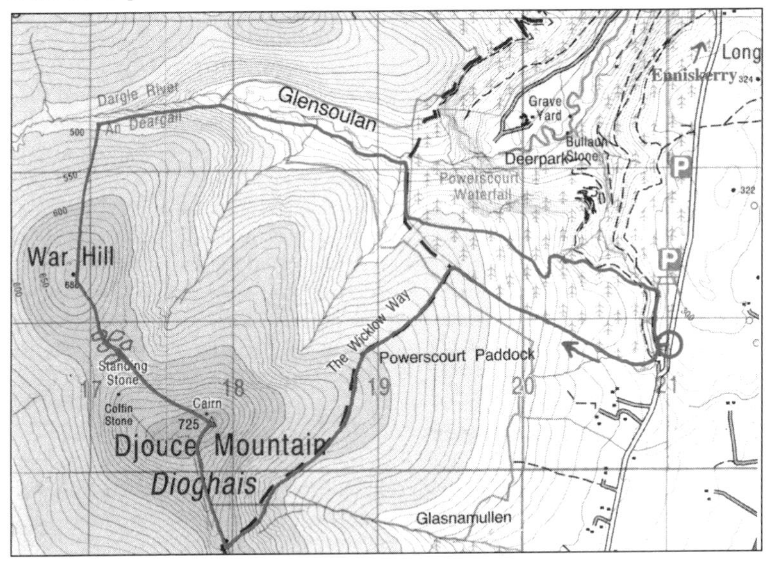

Notes

(1) Grouse House, of which only the chimney stack remains, was once a hunting lodge.

(2) Paddock Pond was a reservoir. In 1986 there was a cloudburst in this area during which waters of the Pond broke through their impounding wall, leaving this low, reedy area. ■

ROUTE 11: BARNACULLIAN RIDGE AND TONELAGEE

Good scenery on the climb onto the broad Barnacullian ridge and really spectacular scenery on the descent from Tonelagee. The ridge walked between these gives excellent long views, but the soft terrain here makes for slow going.

Getting There By car to *Sally Gap*, and thence onward along the Military Road to the large Glenmacnass carpark (GR 114029), about 7 miles to the south. The total distance from central Dublin is about 24 miles.

Walking Time 4 hours (distance 12km, climb 520m).

Difficulties Wet ground on the Barnacullian ridge. On the ridge the Military Road is always somewhere to the east, but so are short stretches of cliff and the far from short and mostly impassable Glenmacnass River. Navigationally therefore, the route requires a little care. At the end of the walk the Glenmacnass River may be difficult to ford, especially after rain. At the start have a look at the providentially placed stones about 70m upstream of the carpark and see if you are going to be able to cross here at the end. (Unfortunately I have no ready solution if you decide you cannot do so.)

Map Sheet 56. Most of the route is on the Glendalough Glenmalur 1:25 000 map.

Route From the carpark walk upstream .... for miles and miles. A riverside walk with the forestry plantations not as oppressive as they appear on the OS map, this stretch gives easy walking and a steady increase in wildness and remoteness. At length (about 5km), you will arrive at the bottom of steep, rock-strewn ground over which the infant Glenmacnass River cascades. Here climb by the stream to the Barnacullian ridge to the west (yes, your premonition was correct).

There is a sudden easing of the slope when you reach the eastern side of the ridge, though it doesn't seem much like a ridge around here – or anywhere else for that matter. Head roughly south to cross a nearby stile in a fence. From here on, keep to this side of the crest of the ridge on a narrow band of grass bordering the large expanse of mud covering the top. Alternatively, there is nothing to prevent your walking boldly down the centre of the ridge, bar the fear of being sucked into the bog, of course. If you do so walk, note that the only indication on the ground of the peak marked on the map as Barnacullian is a signpost, but alas no sign.

South of Barnacullian the ridge narrows slightly and simultaneously dips into a particularly wet area, one where peat hags will cause unwanted detours. Beyond this dip climb directly to Stoney Top (714m), the northern satellite of Tonelagee.

From here the climb to Tonelagee is steep, but navigationally easy on a clear path; the views over Lough Ouler are magnificent. Near the summit note the standing stone overlooking the lough, because from here you can make a steep descent to the lake on the return (see below). Tonelagee (3.25 hours) is one of the finest summits in Wicklow: the third highest at 817m, commanding magnificent views in all directions and with the great corrie containing Lough Ouler gouged out of its north-eastern flank.

From Tonelagee, if you have decided against the direct descent to Lough Ouler described below, take the north-eastern spur to descend steeply, with the heart-shaped lough down on the left. Then climb about 30m to summit 668m. From here a compass bearing of 66° will take you directly down to the carpark across easy, fairly dry ground (my intuition tends to direct me to the right of the correct

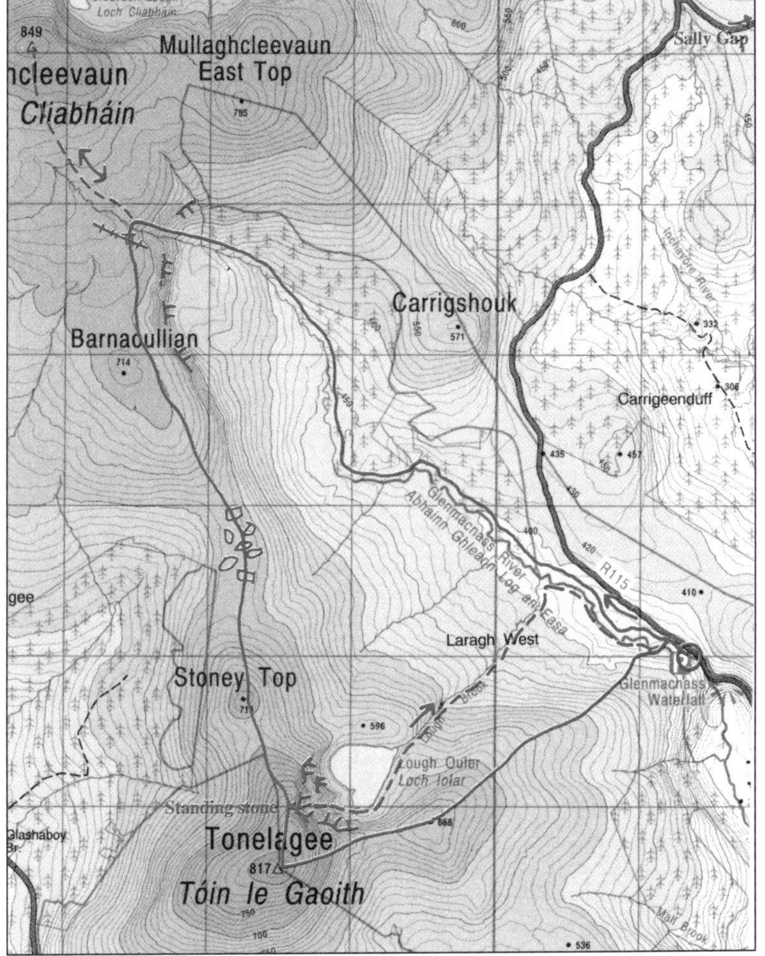

bearing). When you reach Glenmacnass River look out for the stones about 70m upstream of the carpark and cross there.

Mullaghcleevaun Variation When you reach the ridge Mullaghcleevaun is within striking distance, though the deep crevasses in the boggy terrain directly south of the summit make for slow going. Initially keep to the river to minimise peat hags. This variation should take about 1.25 hours.

Steep Descent Variation From the summit of Tonelagee return to the standing stone. From it walk the few metres directly to the cliffs and then look right where there is a grassy gully at your feet. This is the descent route to the lake, and it is here steepest at the top. You can then reach the start by walking along Lough Ouler, its outlet stream and the Glenmacnass River. ■

ROUTE 12: LUGANQUILLIA FROM GLENMALURE

This is only one of several delightful routes from Glenmalure to Lug. A steep climb partly alongside the rapids of the stern Fraughan Rock Glen ends close to the summit, with a return over easy ground giving lovely, long-distance views.

Getting There By car to *Drumgoff crossroads*. Turn right here and drive about another 3 miles, parking in the large carpark at the head of the valley at Baravore (GR 065942). The total distance from Dublin is nearly 40 miles.

Walking Time 5.25 hours (distance 15km, climb 780m).

Difficulties Some attention to navigation required on the descents from Clohernagh and from Art's Lough. Otherwise quite easy, though this is an area with several stretches of cliff so mistakes could be serious.

Map Sheet 56, which shows forest tracks incorrectly, or the Glendalough Glenmalur 1:25 000 map.

Route From the carpark cross the river on a footbridge a little upstream, then turn right onto a tarmac road to reach the youth hostel. Just beyond it, and you are now on a track, turn left uphill onto another track to make a steep climb through trees offering only an occasional glimpse to the stern north-eastern cliffs of Glenmalure. Eventually you will come to a junction with tracks ahead and to the right and a stream close on the left. Take the straight ahead branch which leads you into the heart of the Fraughan Rock Glen with the cliffs of Ben Leagh towering on the right, the steep grassy ground culminating in Cloghernagh on the left and the rapids terminating the end of the Glen ahead. A majestic area.

As you near these rapids you are well beyond private property. Cross the stream and climb by the side of the rapids to reach a soggy valley above. Walk its length, still following the main stream south-westwards, and make your way through boulders upward into an area where the ground is undulating but overall generally rising. Above it, and still to the south-west, lies the plateau crowned by the summit of Lugnaquillia.

Once on the plateau head directly gently uphill over short grass to the huge cairn marking the summit (2.75 hours). At 925m this is the sixth-highest peak in Ireland and the highest in Wicklow. In good weather the views of mountains in all directions are magnificent, those to the north where the great whaleback of Tonelagee is prominent, being particularly fine. Maybe you can see the TV mast on Mount Leinster, about 45km away. This shouldn't be too difficult since a reliable friend (he says he is, anyway) claims to have seen the Reeks, fully 260km away.

From Lug a bearing of 95° compass will take you directly over easy terrain to Clohernagh - or rather, it would if the cliffs of the South Prison didn't intrude. So you can start off on this bearing, veer initially left from it to avoid plunging over the cliffs and shortly after resume it. The scenery on this high-level stretch to Clohernagh is lovely, almost as good as from Lug itself.

Clohernagh (800m) presents only a minor rise, so it is just as well that it has a large cairn. The descent to Art's Lough is a bit tricky navigationally, so in bad visibility it might be prudent to head for the top of the zig-zags (see below). In good weather walk on a compass bearing of about 50° for about 500m to avoid steep ground, then swing left to walk down a grassy ramp to Art's Lough.

The lake is perched on the edge of steep ground running down to Fraughan Rock Glen and overlooked to the south-west by rocky cliffs - a striking location. Curiously, it appears to have no inlet or outlet stream. The latter runs initially underground north-westward to cascade into Fraughan Rock Glen.

The end of a forest track (not marked on sheet 56) is only a few hundred metres north-east of Art's Lough. You can walk directly over high heather to it but in good visibility cross a fence running north on the lake's north-east side to turn left and follow a path. It initially parallels the fence but shortly veers away from it to end at the forest track. And from here it is simply a matter of following the main track downhill, ignoring what are obviously minor tracks. On the valley floor, turn left onto the road and walk 2km back to the carpark.

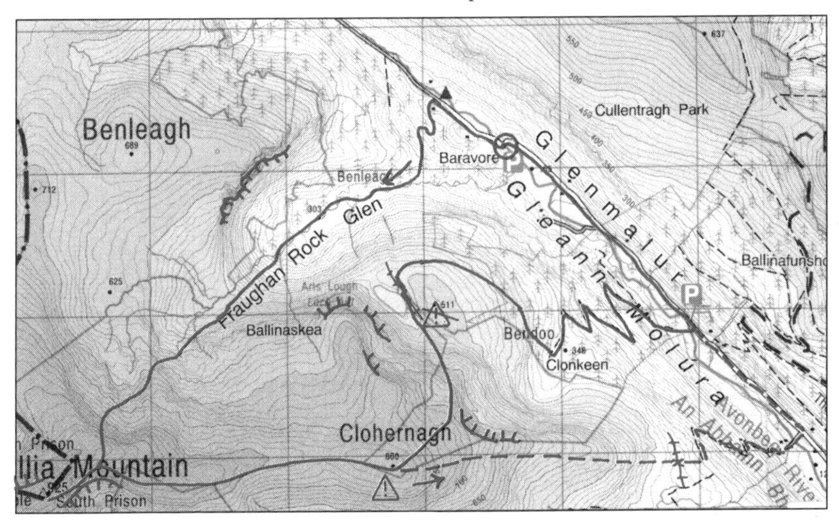

Descent to the Zig-Zags Track Continue east from Clohernagh to walk parallel to the Bendoo cliffs on the left. Farther east cross a fence at a gate, walk directly downhill to shortly pick up a track, indistinct in its higher reaches. If you fail initially to find it, walk downhill keeping the cascades of the Carrawaystick Brook off to the right. Walk by a farmhouse, taking great care to respect the occupiers' privacy, to reach the road. Walking time from Clohernagh to the road is 45 minutes. ■

ROUTE 13: MULLACOR AND CARRIGLINNEEN

A leisurely approach along a side valley of Glenmalure and then above Glenmalure itself to reach lofty but unimpressive Mullacor. Onward across the Military Road to climb rocky Carriglinneen and a descent on track to Glenmalure. A pleasant, undemanding walk with lovely long distance views.

Getting There Drive to *Drumgoff Crossroads*, turn left here and park immediately in the carpark on the right (GR 106908). The owners of the carpark, who run the Glenmalure Lodge opposite, would appreciate your patronage.

Walking Time 5.5 hours (distance 17km, climb 620m).

Difficulties The area around Mullacor is a little featureless and in bad visibility may cause a few anxious moments. The descent from Carriglinneen is through high bracken in summer, when you may like to avoid this area.

Map Sheet 56 or the Glendalough Glenmalur 1:25 000 map.

Route Walk back to the crossroads, turn right and walk uphill to the first forest track on the left. Here take a few seconds to admire the fine stonework in the bridge on the main road and that done, take the right branch of the track, thus keeping on the Wicklow Way, which as a matter of fact, you were on from the beginning.

However at the first junction the Way swings sharply left but you continue straight ahead, still on a forest track, to reach the lower parts of Ballybraid, a secluded, remote but accessible valley, partly forested and partly in fields, in which a few farmhouses nestle. (Yes, it is a slight detour into Ballybraid. I hope you consider it worthwhile.)

At length your forest track wriggles sharply upward through conifers and meets another forest track, your companion for some considerable time to come. Turn left here and walk initially in a wide arc high above the valley carrying the Military Road until you are walking high above Glenmalure itself. The only navigational point you have to remember is to take the left option at the first junction. The views along here are hardly impaired by forestry that is in various stages of growth, but thankfully mostly felled or knee-high. You can therefore enjoy lovely views down into Glenmalure, across to the surging Carrawaystick Waterfall, and beyond it to Lugnaquillia and its attendant peaks.

When you are beyond Carrawaystick Waterfall you will rejoin the Wicklow Way and should fork right uphill with it. (Note: it may be that the route of the Way will change around here. If my directions do not square with it keep on any rising forest track heading north-west and look out for a muddy path heading up through dense forest.) This will take you through a densely forested area, up the muddy path just mentioned and at length into open country on the south-west slopes of Mullacor. Keep on the Way for a little longer, now following boardwalks (walk on them!) until you are at the crest of the ridge with Mullacor to the south-east and the Lugduff ridge to the north-west.

Turn right off the sleepers at the crest to climb the short distance to Mullacor (657m, 3 hours). In spite of its height, Mullacor gives no more than good views to Lugnaquillia to the west, as well as towards Camaderry to the north and the Lugduffs to the north-west. Never mind, the views will be good – and changing – on the eastward leg towards the Military Road.

Descend gently east from Mullacor on an eroded path (in bad visibility note that forest should be on your left) and continue on it, passing the end of the rocky Derrybawn Ridge on the left, to reach a wedge of mature forest on the southern side of one of the undistinguished tops of Cullentragh.

As far as the crest of the Military Road it's forest track – and mostly forest as well – all the way, and though it does not block the views at first you will eventually enter thick trees. At the road you will be relieved to find that you are out of encompassing trees for good.

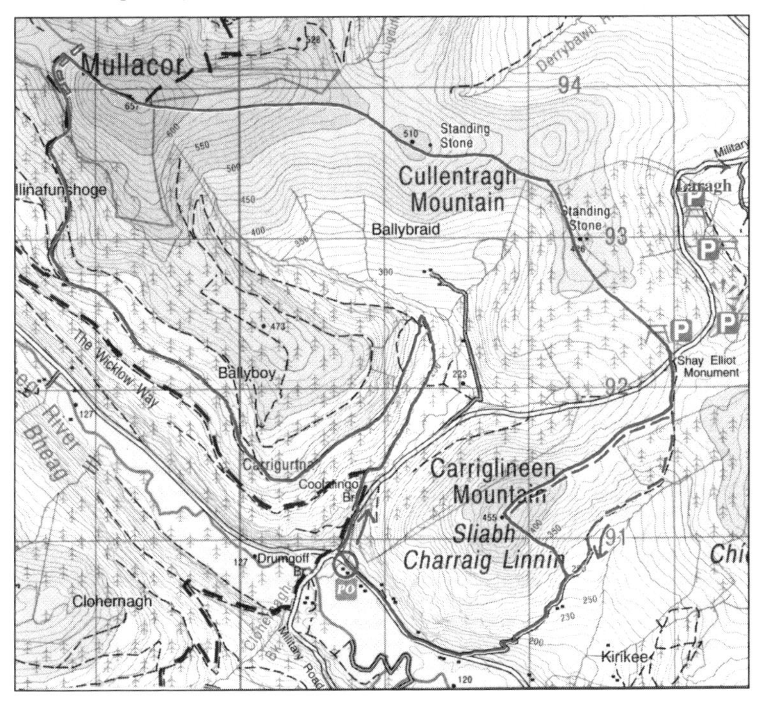

Cross the road here and take the forestry track beyond to the nearby first junction, a slightly offset crosstracks. Turn right here so heading directly for grassy Carriglinneen (455m) to the south-west. Although the forestry track shortly ends there is a path through the rough grass and occasional outcrop to the summit itself, crowned by a modest cairn.

Here a decision. You may not fancy the bracken south-east of Carriglinneen, in which case it may be better to retrace your steps to the crosstracks mentioned earlier, turn right, and make your way south-east from there, branching right at the one fork. Otherwise walk south-east directly from the summit to reach a track bordering fields lower down. Turn right onto it to reach nearby tarmac heading sharply down into Glenmalure. On the main road turn right to walk the kilometre or so back to Drumgoff. ■

ROUTE 14: CROGHAN MOUNTAIN

An isolated hill to the south of the main range, Croghan Mountain (606m) is now threatened with more forestry on its northern slopes, thus reducing further the options for walking. This route is an easy but not over-exciting one with extensive views over field, forest, sea and especially the massed mountains to the north.

Getting There From the village of Aughrim (GR1279), cross the main bridge and turn right. Turn left after over 3 miles, signposted 'Toberpatrick', and left again at the tee. Turn sharply first right, pass two tracks on the left and park on waste ground a few hundred metres farther on (GR 105737) where there is room for a few cars. The total distance from Dublin is 55 miles.

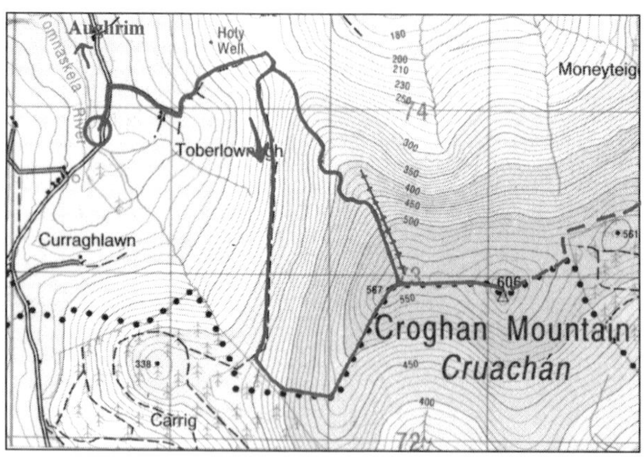

Walking Time 3 hours (distance 8km, climb 480m).

Difficulties None.

Map Sheet 62.

Route Walk back to the first track on the right, by which I mean the first track after alight-ing from the car, take it to a tee (the right branch is over-grown) and turn left uphill. The track is quite muddy so you will probably greet its end close to the crest of the hill with relief.

Turn right here to cross one field and the gate at its corner. Turn right again onto a rough track and take it a few hundred metres downhill to meet a better track running gently uphill south across the face of Croghan. You have now, unfortunately, walked a rough U, uphill and down, to get to a point close to where you were some time previously. However the fences and hedges of the direct approach are too hazardous to attempt.

From here all is easy for heart and foot for a while. Walk the track through young trees and where it enters mature trees take a firebreak upward on an increasingly steep slope. A firebreak may look much like a track but it has none of the track's inhibitions about gradients!

At length you (and the firebreak) reach the crest of the ridge to the south-west of the summit leaving ahead a gentle walk north to summit 567m, a non-event, followed by an equally gentle walk east to the main summit (606m). This is a good stretch to enjoy the views. Among the many mountains to be seen in the main range are the cone of Croaghanmoira to the north with the great corrie of Lugnaquillia's South Prison to its left. A long stretch of coast is also visible; farther along you should be able to see the nearby large coastal town of Arklow.

When you are within a few hundred metres of the summit, and you will see its outcrops protruding from a grassy mound ahead (though hardly its stubby trig pillar), watch out for a junction in the fence you are following, because it marks the descent route. For the moment however continue to the summit.

If you wish you can walk along the summit ridge northwards as far as pt 427m (GR 1475) but then you are going to have to return by the same route or face formidable fences and forest in the lower ground west of Croghan. The main route returns to the junction passed earlier, where you turn north downhill, keeping the fence on your right, as this is the only easy point to cross it.

Follow the fence down through heather and later on a path until you meet a track on the lower slopes. Take it down to the gate crossed earlier, partly cross the field to reach the end of the muddy track and turn onto it to retrace steps all the way back to the start. ■

ROUTE 15: CARRAWAYSTICK AND CROGHANMOIRA

The high points of this route are the sombre beauty of Kelly's Lough and its surrounds, the views from the classical pyramid of Croghanmoira and a delightful stroll along the rocky Fananierin Ridge. Alas, in other parts, views are marred by great expanses of dreary conifers lapping the lower slopes of the hills.

Getting There Drive to *Drumgoff Crossroads*, turn left here and park in the carpark on the right (GR 106908). This is not a public carpark but belongs to the establishment opposite which would welcome, and deserve, your patronage.

Walking Time 6.25 hours (distance 20km, climb 900m). This time, and those given for the variations, are a little less than Naismith's because parts of the route are on easy forest tracks.

Difficulties Navigational care is needed on parts of the route, as indicated below. Underfoot generally good though there is one very wet firebreak.

Maps Sheets 56 and 62, with an awkward transition. Neither shows tracks or forests accurately, so that the Glendalough Glenmalur 1:25 000 map, which does, is a good alternative.

Route From the crossroads take the Wicklow Way south (left) to turn shortly right onto a forest track, a track which winds upwards to reveal much of Glenmalure.

Follow the track round two hairpin bends. At the third, where there is a waymark, take a grassy track on the right heading north-west. After about 10 minutes you will come to a turning circle. Just beyond it the track degenerates to an indistinct path heading upward diagonally right, through the trees. Please follow the path carefully, though a track is only a 100m (distance) or so above you, as you won't want to be lost in forest. After 5 minutes or so the path runs directly upward through a firebreak between mature trees and shortly deposits the possibly relieved walker on a major forest track.

Turn right onto this track and follow it into the valley of the upper Carrawaystick Brook, ignoring one branch heading upward on the left. The views to bulky Cloghernagh over mercifully low trees and the stream gathering its forces

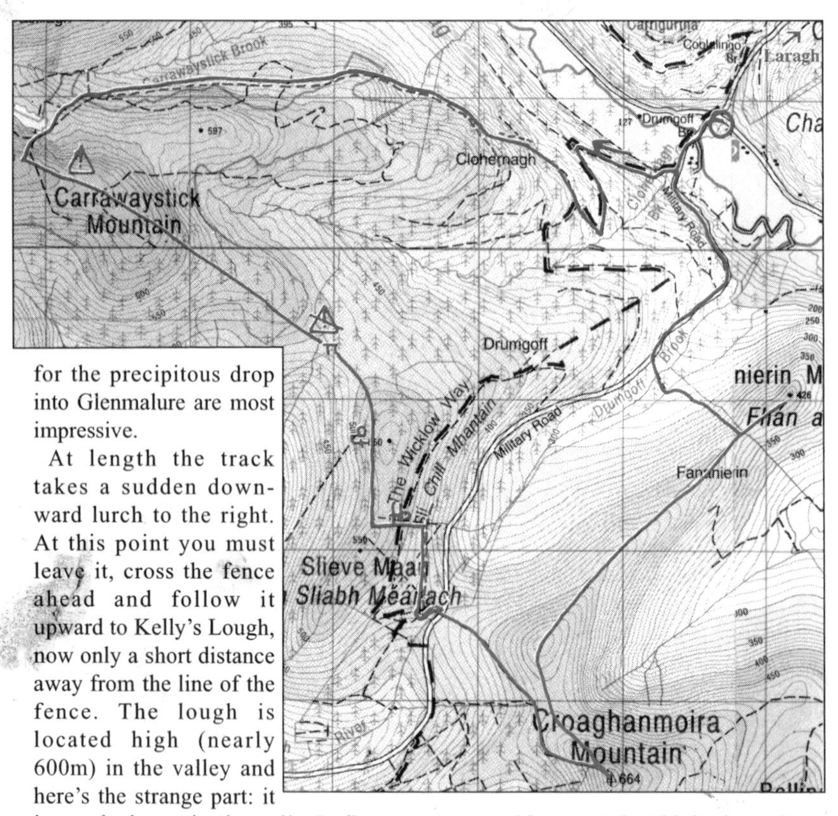

for the precipitous drop into Glenmalure are most impressive.

At length the track takes a sudden downward lurch to the right. At this point you must leave it, cross the fence ahead and follow it upward to Kelly's Lough, now only a short distance away from the line of the fence. The lough is located high (nearly 600m) in the valley and here's the strange part: it is perched, not in the valley's floor as you would expect, but high above it behind a moraine of boulders. It's a lovely location with the crags of Carrawaystick to its left and the valley's end reaching west from it. A good spot for a break (2.25 hours).

That done, return to the near side of the fence and climb to the high haggy ground of Carrawaystick, a spur without a definite summit. The views from about here are magnificent with Kelly's Lough at your feet, Cloghernagh across its valley, the great corrie of the South Prison of Lugnaquillia off to the west and the fine cone of Croghanmoira, the last major peak to be climbed to the south-east. Cross the fence on a stile and just beyond it, and here you are really into peat-hag country, you will come upon a heap of rubbish that few would object to, the pitiful remains of a plane, complete with cross, that crashed here in 1992.

From here on for 2.5km you will have to pay some attention to navigation, which is not helped by the fact that the next target, a stile in a fence with forest beyond, is on sheet 62 (at GR 079894). A compass bearing of about 130° will get you there. There is a rough path through heather but still, check your direction occasionally. Eventually the path passes through young trees following a ditch, and then crosses a forest track. Beyond is the stile.

Cross the stile and follow the firebreak beyond (and fence posts if in doubt) for about 20 minutes. The ground here is exceedingly wet, especially on the initial climb. This, for the record is Slieve Maan. It never was an impressive mountain; now with a dull forest of dull conifers to its summit, it is a most unimpressive.

After the 20 minutes, the firebreak swings gently right and uphill. Turn left here onto a clear firebreak edged by mature dense trees close on both sides. Walk downhill to shortly turn right onto a forest track, with a waymark indicating that this is the Wicklow Way. Navigational troubles are definitely behind.

Follow the Way through trees until it almost reaches tarmac and here leave it to walk to the road – the Military Road at a high pass south of Drumgoff. Cross it and take a grassy track towards Croghanmoira. This is a straightforward climb of about 200m along the track at first, then by forest and finally on a path to the shapely summit (4.5 hours). At 664m, Croghanmoira lies at the edge of the mountains and commands wide views: small wonder that it was chosen as a primary triangulation point for the survey of the country.

From the summit diverge only slightly right from the upward path to climb its bland outlier 1km away to the north-west and then head north-east along the narrow, rocky Fananierin ridge, which gives good views on both sides. At the low point in this ridge you will cross an earthbank which will prove useful for the return. From it, the summit of Fananierin (426m) is only a short distance to the north-east and though it is a there-and-back the views over Glenmalure make it worth the effort. By the way, don't be tempted to head north from Fananierin's summit – it's *very* private. Instead, return to the earthbank, cross it, turn right downhill, and then veer away slightly from it to meet the end of a short stretch of track through forest. At its end is the Military Road again. Turn right onto it to reach Drumgoff Crossroads less than 2km away.

Two Shorter Variations You can easily make two walks out of this route, each taking about 4.5 hours walking time. One is to take the main route almost to the stile mentioned above, turn left onto the forest track here, ignore a track on the left, swing sharply left onto another track and continue downhill until you reach the Wicklow Way which you take initially east. The other is to take the Wicklow Way from Drumgoff to the Military Road and then follow the latter part of the main route. Of the two I would prefer the first. ■

ROUTE 16: TONELAGEE AND GLENMACNASS WOODS

Forest tracks to start giving good glimpses over lower Glenmacnass, followed by a climb above the dramatic corrie of Lough Ouler to lofty Tonelagee (817m). The return gives extensive views along the bumpy Brockaghs.

Getting There By car or St Kevin's bus to *Laragh*. Fork right towards Glendalough in the village, turn right just before McCoy's shop and drive a few hundred metres to park at the forestry entrance on the right.

Walking Time 6 hours (distance 17km, climb 860m).

Difficulties One difficult climb through rocks, though it's avoidable. Moderately difficult navigation on the Brockaghs, whose northern section is quite soggy.

Map Sheet 56 or the Glendalough Glenmalur 1:25 000 map.

Route The start has a lot of junctions in forest tracks so a little attention to detail may be worthwhile, so please bear with me.

Take the track from the forest entrance round a sharp bend to the left and turn right at the first cross-tracks (shown as a simple junction on both maps). Pass a field on the right and ignore a fork on this side immediately after. From now on the track is on a gentle upswing and the mature trees and cleared areas allow good views over Glenmacnass.

Back to boring route finding. Ignore a turn on the left and then a barred grassy track on the right to reach a gate and bar. This point is useful since if you have gone wrong in the course of the previous tedious explanation you can pick up the commentary now. After this the track swings in a gentle, rising arc for over a kilometre before reaching the next junction and a serious decision point. Here you can decide to plod on and upwards for less than 40 minutes to a bridge close to open country or you can make things hard for yourself by dropping about 100m, and then climbing steeply, partly through tough terrain.

Since there is nothing to the easy variation (skip to the next paragraph) we need only look at the difficult one. Descend gently on the track for about 10 minutes to pass a few obviously dead-end tracks and so come to a considerable stream falling here (and indeed above) over broad flat slabs. Because of a dense defence of fallen branches near the stream, keep well to the near side of it at first, so that you will meet what appears to be a firebreak running directly uphill; you will be able to join the stream a little way up. Once you reach it, underfoot conditions improve slightly and you will enjoy the climb to the bridge mentioned above.

After crossing the bridge leave the track to walk upstream for a few metres until you can round a plantation of unhappy looking firs on the right. You cannot remain with these for long: your route lies north-west over a series of bumps reaching towards Tonelagee, dominating the western horizon. Tonelagee is climbed by first tackling a few subsidiary hills, collectively known as Mall Hill, which are all boggy but nonetheless have boulders and even a few precariously perched rocks on their southern flanks.

The last of these subsidiary peaks is summit 668m. Since it overlooks Lough Ouler, a lovely corrie lake backed by the stern grassy cliffs cut into the north-eastern side of Tonelagee, this is a much more memorable peak than its predecessors. There is, as you will readily see, more of this dramatic terrain to come.

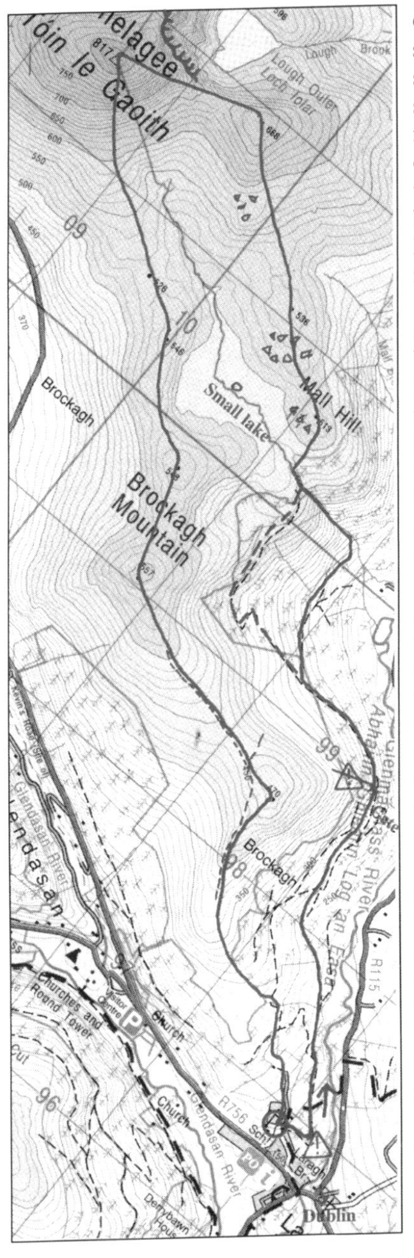

There is a slight drop from summit 668m towards Tonelagee and then a straight and energetic climb to the summit, partly through boulders. The summit itself (817m, 3.75 hours) is marked by a trig pillar and the views embracing Lugnaquillia to the south-west, bumpy Scarr to the east and the broad ridge modestly culminating in Mullaghcleevaun to the north are most impressive.

From Tonelagee descend steeply south-east to the Brockaghs, four bumpy hills reaching down towards Laragh. At the foot of Tonelagee the underfoot conditions change immediately from firm to soggy on an intermittent, eroded path. Here it might help navigation to note that there is a small lake about 500m east of the northern (546m) Brockagh.

Climb the first three Brockaghs (summits 546m, 548m, 557m) and then swing nearly east towards the fourth (470m), now on a much clearer path. As you approach the rock-strewn summit of 470m you will join a wider track onto which you turn right. It's worth leaving the track to climb to the summit; you can pick it up again just to its south.

Rejoin this track to meet a set of fences. After it, keep close to young trees on the left and you will be channelled downhill east through a narrow gap and onto a forest track, where you turn right.

The rest is easy. Take the track to a nearby tee, and here cross the gate you will see directly ahead. Walk along a grassy path leading around a deserted house to your right. Beyond it continue downhill, now back on a track, to reach the forest entrance where you started. ■

ROUTE 17: GLENDASAN, CAMADERRY AND GLENEALO

A lovely, undemanding walk taking in the two valleys on either side of Camaderry. Both valleys are attractive, with Glenealo one of the best, if not the best in Wicklow. Between them, Camaderry offers excellent long-range views (of course), though Turlough Hill's Upper Reservoir does not enhance them.

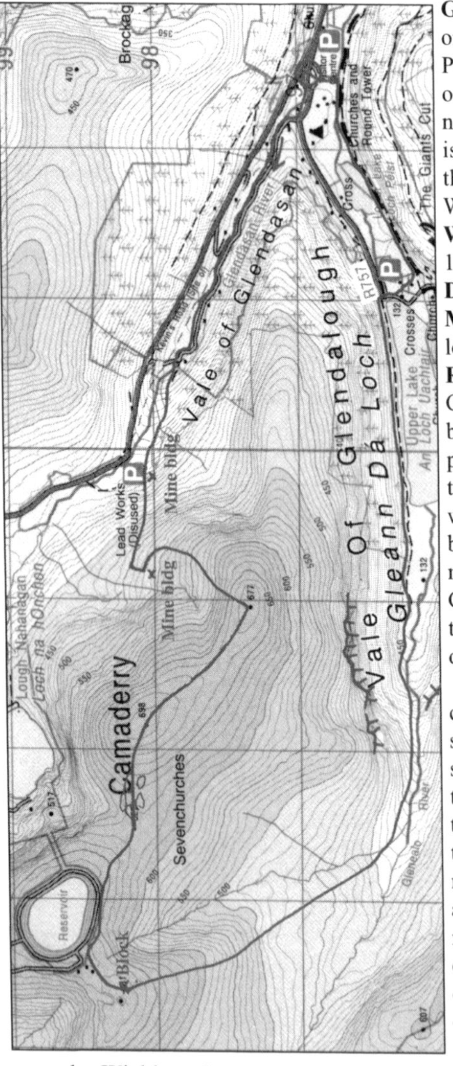

Getting There By St Kevin's bus or car to *Glendalough* (GR 1296). Park in the Visitor Centre to avoid overcrowding in the village, but note its closing time. The Centre is on the left just after you pass the junction on the right for the Wicklow Gap.

Walking Time 5 hours (distance 15km, climb 640m).

Difficulties None.

Map Sheet 56 or the Glendalough Glenmalur 1:25 000 map.

Route On leaving the Visitor Centre, turn left to cross the main bridge in the village. Continue past the Round Tower and then take the next turn right, a track, which immediately leaves tourist-bound Glendalough to enter a more tranquil world with the Glendasan River on the right and the rising shoulder of Camaderry on the left.

From here on for some considerable time navigation is simple: in brief keep the river somewhere on the right and keep to any path or track that facilitates this. This route will take you through the occasional abandoned mine working (not all that hideous a blot on the landscape) to the ruins of a fine mine building, certainly not an ordinary dwelling. Here take a path that continues diagonally upward in a straight line to give good views over the Wicklow Gap road and towards bulky Tonelagee. This path finally swings left and left again at right angles (there are the remains of yet another mine building at the second) before expiring in high heather with the gently rounded south-east summit of Camaderry a not too strenuous climb to the south. This summit (677m, 2 hours) is crowned by a fine cairn and from it, it is only a short walk over easy ground to the slightly higher north-west summit (698m), also gently rounded but with only a rudimentary cairn, unusual for Wicklow.

We now directly face the ramparts of the Upper Reservoir of Turlough Hill. From the north-west summit descend into peat hags and then climb slightly to reach a rough path close by the perimeter fencing, the ramparts on the right. Then head on a track for an ugly concrete block just to the south-west of the Upper Reservoir. Ugly though it be, it is a convenient point from which to start the next stage, an easy one into the valley of Glenealo.

There is a long spur of high land reaching south-east from the building and it forms a nice lofty route into Glenealo. Just in case you are wondering however, it is possible to reach Glenealo from *any* point around here at the building. When you meet the main stream in the valley all your navigational problems, such as they were, are over: turn left and keep walking downstream. This is a lovely stretch: a high remote valley here in Upper Glenealo, the great cliffs and boulders of Camaderry (left) and the Spink (right) overlooking the Upper Lake farther down. At about these mighty portals you will pick up a path, later a zig-zag track which will take you down to the floor of the main valley.

Above the shores of the Upper Lake is a wide track, popular with day-trippers. Take it to its far end, cross the end of the Upper Lake to reach the woods bordering the southern side of the narrow valley. Walk the track here past the Lower Lake and then cross the second footbridge on the left over the Glendasan River to reach the Visitor Centre carpark. ■

ROUTE 18: DERRYBAWN AND THE SPINK

A short walk, though you can easily extend it, in some of the most magnificent country in Wicklow: Derrybawn and the Spink are both narrow, rocky ridges and both offer varying panoramas over lovely mountain scenery.

Getting There Car to the Upper Carpark *Glendalough* about a mile beyond the village. Bus to the St Kevin's bus terminus from where you can walk along the wooded southern side of the valley to the start proper.

Walking Time 4 hours (distance 10km, climb 680m).

Difficulties Normally only a little wet underfoot. Navigation is easy.

Map Sheet 56. The National Park and the Glendalough Glenmalur 1:25 000 sheets also cover the route and show paths and tracks better than sheet 56.

Route From the carpark walk south to cross a sward and beyond it take a path upward beside the surging Pollanass Waterfall. At the top of the path continue on a track for a short distance, then turn first left to cross two nearby closely spaced bridges. So far, so easy.

Sterner stuff lies ahead. Just past the bridges take a path on the right heading diagonally upward roughly south-east through young trees (there are several vague paths here). It crosses a forest track and, now quite distinct, continues straight and steeply up beyond it through mature trees to emerge from forest into open ground just west of Derrybawn. Continue upward, still on the path to the summit cairn (474m).

All the while from the start the scenery has been good and ever widening. And now from the summit onward a wide panorama of high mountains is revealed in all directions, a panorama that will be enhanced in the walk ahead.

From the summit walk south-west along the narrow, rocky Derrybawn ridge, the finest in Wicklow, though admittedly Wicklow is not particularly noted for its ridges. At its end after about 1.5km cross the end of a rough track to face moorland. Now walk to the left-most corner of mature trees 500m or so to the west, to which there is a rough path.

At this corner follow a fence away from forest to reach a convenient place to cross it and then head towards the summit of Mullacor, a path and short grass making for easy going. This section is gently upward all the way except for one level area, which you should not confuse for the summit in bad visibility. It (657m, 2.5 hours) is also flat, but has an unmistakable drop after it.

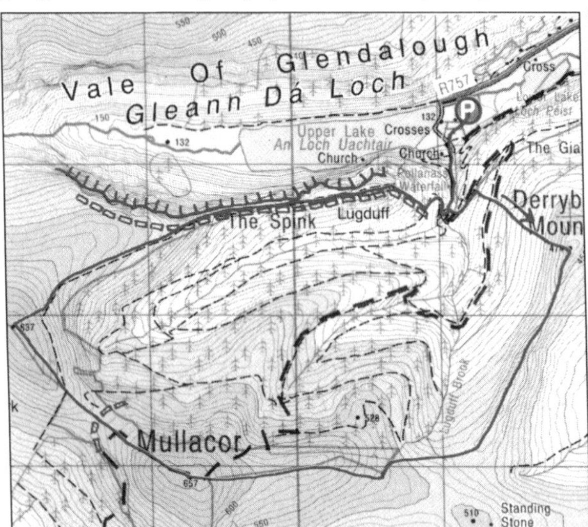

From Mullacor walk downhill north-west to a grassy col crossed by a boardwalk and then climb to Lugduff East (637m). This is the point at which you can decide to extend the walk (see below). If you don't want to, head north-east from the summit to turn left onto a wide firebreak (or maybe it is a track) bordering an expanse of forest in various stages of growth.

From here on navigation is simple and you can concentrate on some of the finest views in the entire mountain area. Simply keep to the track, which gradually narrows to a path and then to a boardwalk running east along the Spink and high above the Upper Lake. Along the Spink the cliffs overlooking Glendalough are at your feet with others facing you across the deep, narrow valley to its north, while on the other side a fringe of trees fronts a partly wooded upland valley.

The walk along the Spink is about 2km long, and is spectacular all the way. Towards its end the boardwalk will direct you right steeply downhill through trees to a forest track. Turn left onto it to reach the track junction, which you should recognise from earlier in the day. Turn left and walk downhill to the carpark.

Longer Variation From Lugduff East you can continue along the Lugduff ridge to the col at GR 0596 facing Conavalla. From there you can descend to Glenealo River, cross it and walk all the way downhill into Glendalough. The walking time from Lugduff East is 2.25 hours. ■

ROUTE 19: CIRCUIT OF GLEN OW

A long walk with lovely views and fairly good ground underfoot, especially in the centre section, much of which is over 600m. However, it's a pity that there is so much forestry to start. Unusually for Wicklow nearly all the climbing is before and all the descent after the highest point of the day, Lugnaquillia.

Getting There A long 42 miles from Dublin, much of it over bad or indifferent roads. Drive to *Drumgoff crossroads,* continue south for nearly 6 miles, here forking right. Pass the large building that was, and will be again, Aghavannagh youth hostel, and park shortly beyond at the forestry entrance on the right (GR 055862).

Walking Time 6.25 hours (distance 18km, climb 850m).

Difficulties Navigation generally easy, though make sure that you reach open country on the ascent and that you descend the correct spur after Lugnaquillia. Do not attempt the walk in the opposite direction as this makes route finding much more difficult.

Map Sheets 56 and 62, with an easy transition. Forestry and forestry tracks are particularly badly shown on sheet 62. The alternative is the Glendalough Glenmalur 1:25 000 map, which is generally accurate in its depiction of forestry, though I still find it hard to reconcile part of the upward route even with this map.

Route Take the track at the forestry entrance and, ignoring a minor turn on the right which ends at a house, fork first right after 700m or so. This takes you through a region of high trees with only the occasional view so it will be some consolation to reach a tee and the prospect of more interesting terrain.

At the tee turn right (alternatively it can be described as straight ahead) and almost immediately leave the track to take a wide firebreak running directly uphill and carrying a stream. Cross a forest track and continue onward and upward until you are into rough heather following a firebreak and a set of ancient fence poles.

Eventually you will find the firebreak and poles heading roughly north-east, with your way ahead barred by young trees. It is at this point that the 1:25 000 map doesn't make much sense, but no matter. Turn sharply left (north-west) here, still following a firebreak and fence poles along the crest of a gently rising spur.

After crossing several fences in various stages of antiquity, you will come to a less decrepit fence and a set of parallel ditches marking the line of the highest forest. From here head north-east (the exact direction is luckily not vital, which is just as well because you are crossing the border from sheet 62 to 56). This will take you onto the high ground to the south of Kelly's Lough and to the start of the most memorable section of the walk.

Turn left when you reach the edge of steep ground plunging north towards the lough; there is no mistaking it. With the lake far below and the shoulder of Clohernagh beyond it, this is a lovely stretch whose scenery is sustained until well after Lugnaquillia, 3km to the west.

Corrigasleggaun (794m), crowned by a humble cairn, is the first peak to be climbed, after which there are renewed views of Kelly's Lough, now considerably further below. From Corrigasleggaun drop to the north-west and then resume the climb by joining another spur, that from Clohernagh, which comes in from the right.

As you face west towards Lugnaquillia, you are walking a gently sloping terrain of short grass, high above the bulk of the Wicklow mountains, with magnificent views in all directions. A general bearing west should suffice, though near the summit keep well clear of the South Prison, as it is easy enough to wander down when you encounter steep ground initially, though the cliffs nearer the summit are sheer and therefore unmistakable.

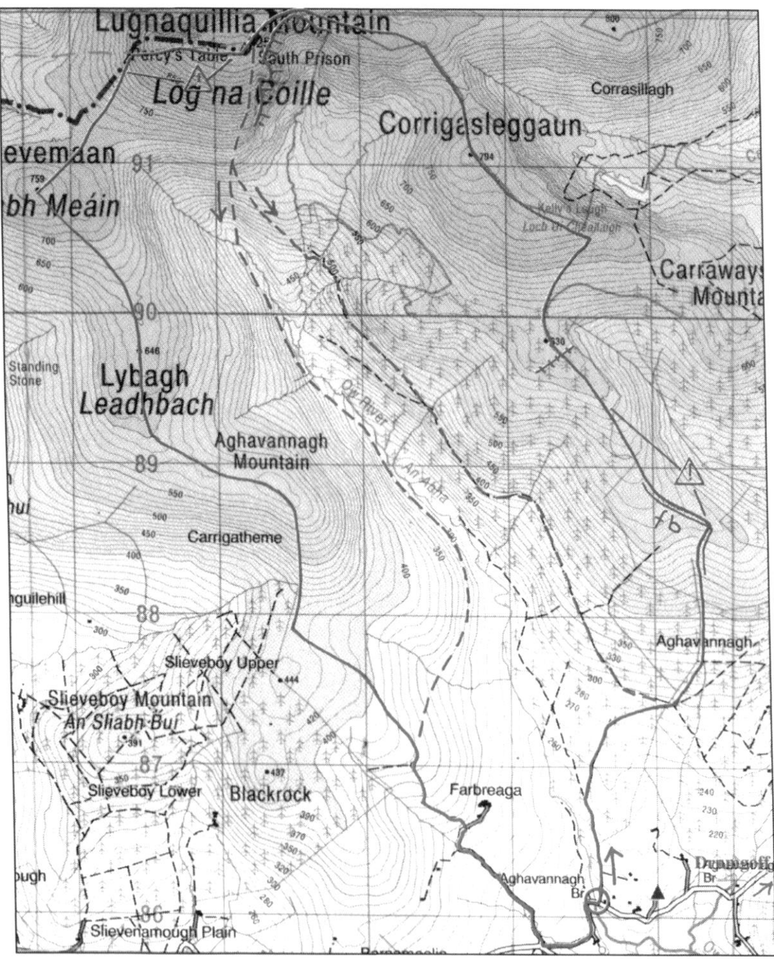

Lugnaquillia (925m, 3.75 hours) has a most unimpressive summit, an almost flat level plain of short grass, with a huge cairn at its centre. However walk only a few metres to north or south and the full majesty of your location immediately becomes apparent. To the north, overlooking the cliffs of the North Prison, is a wide panorama of mountains of which whale-backed Tonelagee is the most impressive. To east and west is high, unforested ground, while to the south, overlooking the South Prison, the mountains are lower, though the TV mast on Mount Leinster, the highest mountain in the Blackstairs, should be clearly visible in good weather. If in doubt as to the location of any feature you can refer to the mountain indicator a few metres from the cairn.

From the summit walk west to the edge of the summit plateau and then descend steep rock-strewn ground. Then swing south-west thus heading away from the enticing spur towards Camarahill. This south-west gentler descent ends in a flotilla of peat hags and wet ground from where Slievemaan (759m) is a short but stiff climb (you can circumvent the summit if you wish by passing it on its east side). The leg from Slievemaan passes back over onto sheet 62 with the not so inviting prospect of reaching a peak (Lybagh) with no discernible summit, not even a cairn. In bad weather take a compass bearing of about 152° for 1.5km to reach it; in good weather swing initially left of this bearing to keep to the high ground. The views along here are dramatic: unfortunately the best are behind you where the jaws of the South Prison yawn not altogether benignly.

The next peak, Aghavannagh Mountain (over 580m), is more accommodating navigationally, since a slight rise presages it and what is more, a line of fencing begins at the summit. Simply follow the fence downhill to a block of forest and follow the forest for a few hundred metres before veering away from it to reach a rough track (you can head directly for the track but you will encounter bog workings if you do).

Once on the track the rest is easy. Take it down south-eastward through upland fields to another track, this one comparatively major, turn right onto it and follow it to tarmac at a tee. Turn left for the nearby start.

Escape/Shorter Variation Admittedly not much of an escape route nor much shorter, but since it is in forest it may offer some shelter in bad weather. From the summit of Lugnaquillia descend steeply south with the cliffs of the South Prison close on the left (excellent views!) and so reach the corner of forest at GR 036906. Walk another few hundred metres south along the forest edge to a stile and a clear path beyond heading into the forest. From here it is an easy walk to the start.

Ow Valley Variation You may prefer to walk the Ow Valley rather than the not very inspiring peaks from Slievemaan to Aghvannagh. If so take the above variation but do not enter the forest. Instead continue down the valley and when faced by fences ahead veer uphill away from the river. Climb to the track mentioned at the end of the main route and take that route to the start. ■

ROUTE 20: CONAVALLA AND CAMENABOLOGUE

A route in a spectacular area taking in the remote end of Glenmalure and some of the peaks surrounding that valley. Not an easy route to follow as the summits are not the most distinct, so keep this route for a clear day.

Getting There Drive to *Drumgoff crossroads*, turn right here and continue for 3 miles to near the end of the valley at Baravore where there is a large carpark (GR 065942).

Walking Time 5.25 hours (distance 14km, climb 780m).

Difficulties As stated, not a route for days of poor visibility as the navigation is not easy and there are some areas of cliff and impenetrable forest around. Underfoot conditions generally good.

Map Sheet 56 or the Glendalough Glenmalur 1:25 000 map.
Route From the carpark walk a few metres upstream on a path (I won't mention the ugly ford), and cross the Avonbeg River by a footbridge. On the opposite bank turn right onto a road and walk as far as the youth hostel. Cross back over the river here on a bridge and then make a decision.

If it is the height of summer the bracken will be luxuriant upstream and the intermittent path you have to follow will be obscured. Under these circumstances it would be as well to ascend out of the valley bottom as soon as possible. Otherwise, and this is in spite of an area of gorse to be endured shortly, you can enjoy a pleasant walk upstream.

In high summer therefore start climbing steeply north-eastwards, avoiding the occasional outcrop and gully until you are into less steep, grassy country. The climb should take at least 30 minutes and you may have to rely on this time as the change in slope is not all that obvious. When you are into this gently sloped ground contour north-west until you encounter a stream with forest beyond it and maybe a triangle of forest creeping up the slope close below you. Wait here until those following the valley route rejoin you!

For the valley route walk upstream to shortly reach a path that leads through a painful area of high gorse (it lasts only a few hundred metres but might seem considerably longer). Emerging from this purgatory you will attain a heavenly area beyond it with the Avonbeg River plunging over rocks. You will find that it is easier to walk somewhat above the river as there is an intermittent path here; this

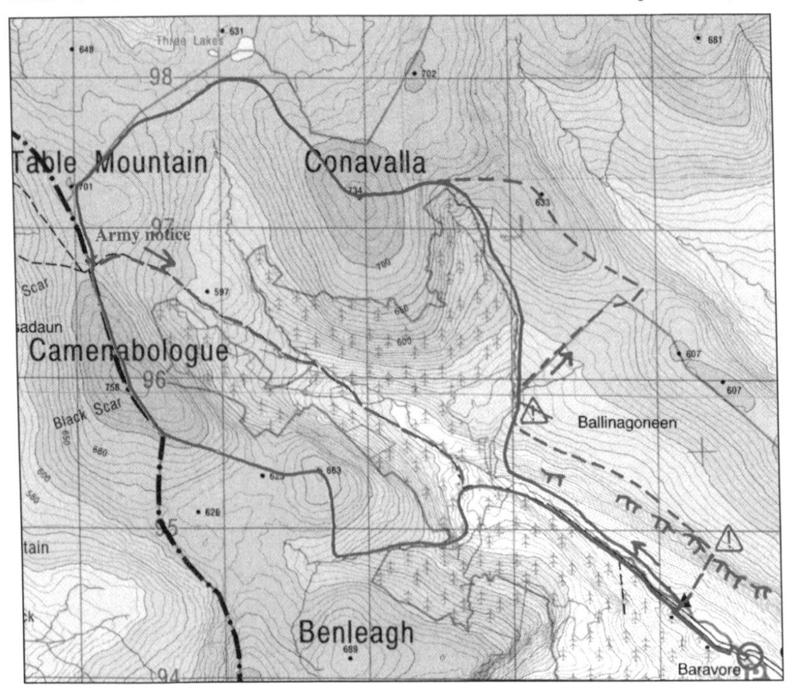

also lessens slightly the pain of the real ascent to come. At length you will reach a tributary stream with dense forest beyond it. Climb here to reach the same point as those who took the alternative route.

The idea now is to follow roughly the extensive forestry plantations on the left but if you feel confident you can aim away from them by walking north-east to reach a col at GR 0596 lying between the Lugduffs and Conavalla. Pick up the main route on Conavalla's summit.

However let's say you follow the forest. Keep it within reach until it swings sharply away downhill and then walk the remaining short distance west to Conavalla's summit (734m). Conavalla is unfortunately a dumpy, unprepossessing mountain, a plateau-like summit of stony soil and the odd peat hag.

From Conavalla head north-west over moorland towards Three Lakes of which curiously, there are two. Three Lakes serve the useful function of being unmistakeable landmarks. There is no need to reach their soggy shores; instead curve towards them and then head south-west to Table Mountain (701m), another undistinguished peak though with a prominent cairn, the only indication of a summit. From here head south to the nearby highest point of the track running between the Glen of Imaal and Glenmalure, here quite nebulous, so that the Army notice and sheltering wall, a good spot for a break, are helpful in locating your position (3.25 hours).

You can shorten the route here by heading initially east but after that south-east downhill into Glenmalure, a simple route on track all the way, taking about 1.25 hours. Otherwise head south through good ground with the occasional peat hag to Camenabologue (758m), a fine high peak giving excellent views, of which the Lugnaquillia massif to the south and the great mound of Tonelagee to the north-east are the most prominent.

From Camenabologue keep to the path on high ground following its south-east spur but where this path shortly swings away south towards far-off Lugnaquillia keep on roughly south-east heading for the undistinguished summit 663m. From here descend south to reach a narrow valley carrying a stream, on whose other side is dense forest. Turn left downstream and say farewell to navigational and hello to underfoot problems.

This is a lovely stretch it's a pity that you will not be able to concentrate for long on its pools and tiny waterfalls as it makes its swirling progress into Glenmalure. The problem is that you soon enter a stretch of mature forest in which there has been felling and this makes for a difficult, steep descent. The only advice I can offer is to keep the stream on the right and to say that you will reach a track in a few minutes.

Once on the track, which runs high above the floor of Glenmalure in a partly clear-felled area, the rest is easy. Turn left, shortly ignore a track branching off to the left and take the next turn right. This is the ancient track up the length of the valley, as you will recognise from the sett of the stones. This will take you shortly out of trees, leaving a pleasant walk back down into Baravore. ■

ROUTE 21: SORREL HILL TO BALLYKNOCKAN

The road which runs along the eastern shore of Pollaphuca Reservoir is lined with farmland which can be easily crossed in only a few places. The main route therefore is a linear one requiring two cars. It traverses muted peaks that offer good views west over the reservoir and towards more distinctive mountain country in other directions.

Getting There You will need one car at the finish in the carpark on the left just before entering the village of Ballyknockan (GR 010073). The route starts at a forest entrance (GR 003123) off the road to *Lackan*. To get there cross the reservoir, continue towards Lackan for about 1$^1/_2$ miles, turning left here onto a narrow cul de sac road, and so described. Drive a short distance to the forest entrance. If there are many cars in your party it might be better to park on the main road.

Walking Time 5.25 hours (distance 15km, climb 720m).

Difficulties Unless you are quite confident (and able) don't attempt this route in bad visibility as there is difficult navigation after Black Hill. However in an emergency you can head west to the road. Enough wet ground to satisfy the most demanding duck.

Map Sheet 56.

Route Take the forest track, turning left off it at the first clear firebreak - it doesn't matter if you miss it as there are several clear passages. Cross two tracks to emerge on the crest of the spur named Lugnagun.

Once there, turn right to face Sorrel Hill. This is a pleasant, easy stretch: good ground underfoot, forest and later an earthbank to take care of navigational worries, and fairly good views in all directions.

The earthbank continues onto the lower slopes of Sorrel, after which the climb to the summit is easy. Sorrel (599m) is crowned by a huge cairn on an eroded area of rock and sand. The views are good: Seahan and Seefingan to the north-east with a whole line of gently moulded peaks culminating diffidently in Mullaghcleevaun on the southern horizon.

It is towards Mullaghcleevaun that we must now face. Descend south to reach a minor road and carpark at Ballynultagh Gap, from where take the bog road southwards to its end near the summit of Black Hill (602m, 2.75 hours). Walk the remaining distance to the summit, an unshapely upturned pudding bowl.

Navigation from here on is quite difficult on gently sloping, featureless terrain and with a turning point in the middle of nowhere. In good weather you can descend south-east from Black Hill, skirt round the soggy headwaters of Ballynastockan Brook and then climb Moanbane. In bad visibility (and let's hope you aren't there in such conditions), a compass bearing directly from Black Hill to Billy Byrne's Gap might be the best bet; you will notice the steady if unspectacular drop into Glenbride if you begin to overshoot it.

At the Gap climb steadily west to the summit plateau of Moanbane (703m), where a north-south oriented lake about 7 double-steps across marks the vague summit, an admittedly meagre landmark. The next target is Silsean (698m) to the south-west, Moanbane's twin sister and no more notable than Moanbane. Just to the east of its summit plateau is a useful landmark: an acute junction of two fences.

From Silsean descend directly north-west and when, far down the slope you encounter forest (not shown on the map) keep it on the right to reach a gate with a road beyond it and beyond that again untidy quarry workings. Take this road down to Ballyknockan, ignoring lots of side roads ending at houses or the quarry.

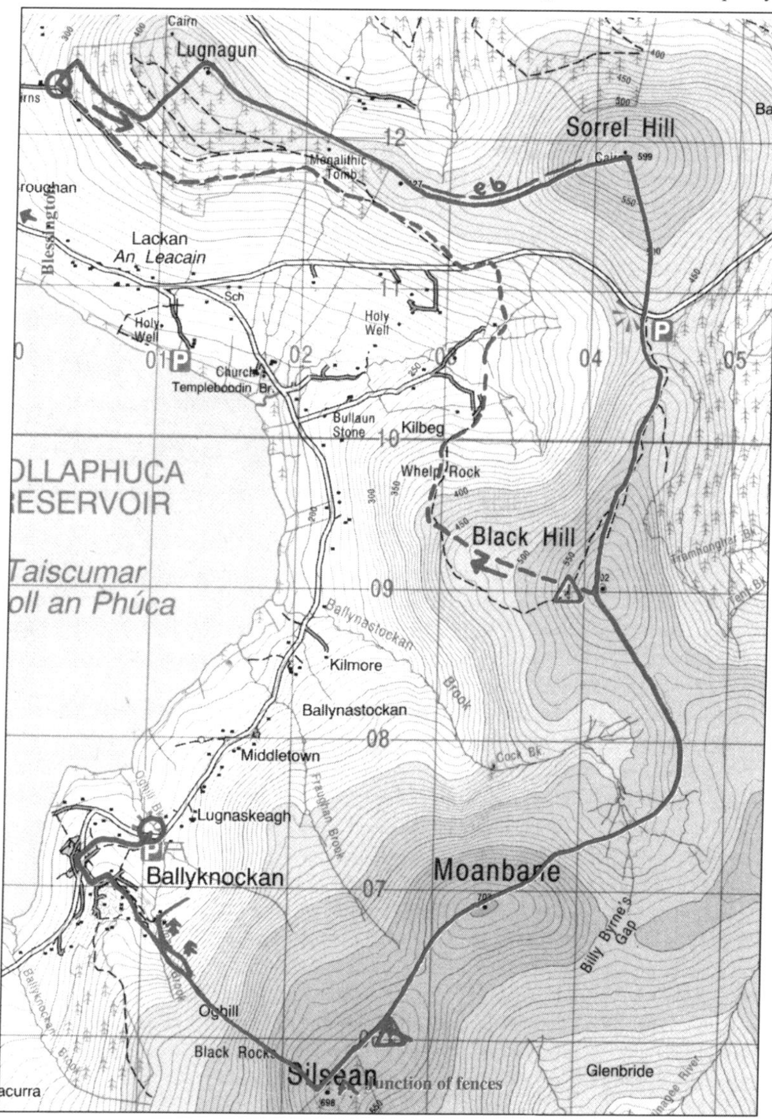

In the village turn right, take the immediate turn on the right and walk directly back to the car park.

One Car or Bus Variation (You can get the bus to Blessington for this variation.) Take the main route to the summit of Black Hill, descend north-west to pick up a grassy track. Turn right onto it to reach a large complex of buildings surrounded by a rectangular fringe of trees. Turn right to walk round one side of this fringe, then head north to the road. Turn left here, keep on the road for a few hundred metres, then leave it to climb gently through open country walk and cross a gate at a forest edge about 100m from its lower end. Take the left branch here, walk directly to the start. Total walking time is 5.5 hours (distance 17km, climb 660m).

ROUTE 22: LOBAWN AND CORRIEBRACKS

Do not be deceived: the miles of moorland that you will see as you start this route conceal more miles of moorland that you cannot see. Nevertheless, the long views are varied and occasionally spectacular and there is the satisfaction of finding your way round some of the most featureless terrain in Wicklow.

Getting There A long 30 miles from Dublin. Take the N81 past *Blessington*, about 6 miles beyond it turn left onto the R756, drive for 3.0 miles and here turn right (the second of two adjacent turns). Drive 2.2 miles and park at a track on the left (the second of two adjacent tracks on this side) (GR 980003). The last 2.2 miles are narrow so try to avoid taking a convoy of cars along this road.

Walking Time 4.25 hours (distance 12km, climb 550m).

Difficulties The featureless terrain means that navigation is not the easiest. Nonetheless, the few small landmarks are reassuring and even if you fail to find them the surrounding terrain is not hazardous if you keep clear of forests.

Map Sheet 56. Its depiction of forest is better than usual for these maps.

Route Take the track from the parking place to shortly cross a stream, the infant Douglas River. This track swings left in a wide arc to pass between, on the left, an almost flat pancake (called Round Hill on the map) and on the right pt 511m (called Round Hill by the walking fraternity, and not quite your initial goal). After 20 minutes or so the track has degenerated to a line of reeds so you might as well abandon it and instead keep the several tributaries of the Douglas River on the right as you ascend roughly east through short heather towards Round Hill.

You are likely to hit Round Hill at a small cairn a little south of forest and a little north of pt 511m, which seems to have no corporeal existence. After admiring the view north over the Wicklow Gap Road, head south along a gently sloped spur towards pt 599m, 2km away across featureless terrain that at least has the grace to offer easy going and good views of two similar spurs to east and west.

You are not going to be able to find pt 599m, another incorporeal entity, but you should see, just to the east, a small area of disturbed ground and beyond it a clear ditch heading south-east to Table Mountain. (In bad visibility you will observe if you go too far south that the slight upward incline from pt 511m gives way to an equally slight downward decline.) From here on to beyond Lobawn, by the way, the views to the south over the Glen of Imaal and beyond it to Lugnaquillia and the great corrie gouged out of its flank, are most impressive.

From pt 599m head west keeping to the high ground and following a continuation of the ditch already seen heading south-east. This route will take you over a small but distinct summit, pt 563m, down to Cavanagh's Gap and then upward again to the highest point of the day, Lobawn (636m, 2.75 hours), which is crowned by a short pillar bearing the abbreviation WD13, so you can't mistake it. Lobawn is a none too impressive mountain, but it has a pleasant grassy spur to the south, one which shortly swings abruptly west, and another less capricious grassy spur directly to the west, whither we are bound.

Keep to this western spur for about 10 minutes, at which point you should see a few forlorn fence posts off to the right marking the highest ambition (not quite

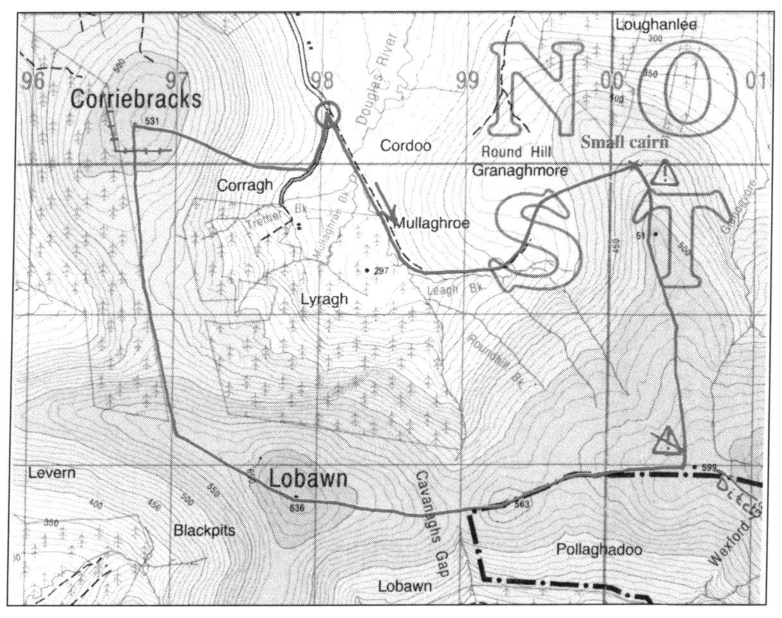

achieved) of the forestry authorities. Turn right here (north) keeping forestry a little lower down on the left. This course will take you down to a broad col from which you can start the climb, still roughly north, to Corriebracks. As you ascend you will note that the forestry edge swings away to north-west, this in spite of the opinion of the map to the contrary. You will cross a rusty fence just before the summit (531m), a good indication of its imminence, and one that you might be thankful for in the absence of any notable feature on the summit plateau.

The descent is roughly east over high vegetation, the only such of the day. This reveals for the first time the valley where you started: a nice mixture of fields, groups of trees and the occasional farmstead. Aim a little to the south of the starting place. This will take you down past, to the right, stone walls enclosing upland fields: at the time of writing this appears to be the best way to access the road but you may have other ideas. Once on it turn left for the start which is about 5 minutes away. ■

ROUTE 23: LOUGHS NAHANAGAN AND FIRRIB

A dificult climb by Lough Nahanagan onto one of the summits of Camaderry is rewarded by views far and near. From here to Lough Firrib underfoot conditions are generally boggy, and the continuing long panoramas are a little marred by the walls of Turlough Hill reservoir. The walk ends in a delightful, remote valley.

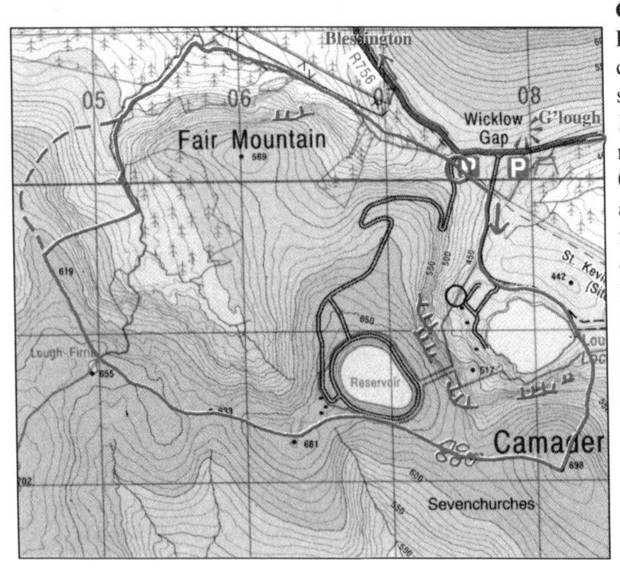

Getting There Park in the *inner* carpark at the summit of the *Wicklow Gap* road (GR 075002). You can also drive there from *Blessington* on the N81 and R756. The start is nearly 40 miles from Dublin.

Walking Time 4 hours (distance 11km, climb 500m), including about 15 minutes over Naismith for difficult terrain.

Difficulties Wet underfoot for much of the route. Navigation in the centre section around Lough Firrib is quite demanding so you might have anxious moments on a bad day.

Map Sheet 56 or the Glendalough Glenmalur 1:25 000 map. On the former several of the small streams you are going to need for navigation are completely obscured by the green line used for the National Park boundary.

Route From the carpark walk south-east on a path following a series of iron goal posts from near the start. This will take you to the lower power station road onto which you turn right. You can keep on it to what appears to be a jetty projecting into Lough Nahanagan at the end of the road or you can refuse such comfort and cross elevated bogland to arrive at the 'jetty'.

From here Camaderry lies to the south, the direct route barred by cliff forming the corrie behind Lough Nahanagan, while to the left is an occasional crag. Make your way through these crags, thus not quite directly heading to the summit of Camaderry (698m). Veer farther left if the ground is too steep, though there is little you can do to avoid high heather of the lower slopes.

As you gain height the vegetation becomes much easier. The summit itself, the north-west of Camaderry's two, is a plateau of rock and soft ground. From here bulky Tonelagee looms across the valley to the north, hummocky Scarr is to the north-east and the Lugnaquillia massif dominates the skyline to the south-west.

Descend west into a haggy col and then climb slightly onto the southern side of the giant ramparts of Turlough Hill, one of the few features in the Wicklow mountains that you simply cannot mistake (1.75 hours). Which is just as well because you will have to be sure of your starting point to find the next target, the reclusive Lough Firrib.

Walk to the quarry just to the south-west of Turlough Hill, which you will recognise since it is guarded by a pathetically inadequate fence. From here you can take a bearing of 298° compass to Lough Firrib, though you will have to make a few detours to avoid crags on what is predominantly wet and boggy ground.

The small lake lies in undulating moorland and so you will come across it only when you are very close. Here a sigh of relief may be in order before you set off on the next leg. (By the way if you fail to find Lough Firrib do not despair. It's only a short leg from the quarry so if you have paid attention to your Naismith timing you won't be too far out and can set off on the next leg knowing you must be at its approximate location.)

This leg is along the broad spur to the north-west. I have chosen a quite convoluted route simply because I like the valley to the spur's north-east. This route makes navigation a little harder and means a steeper descent so you may elect to walk to the far end of the spur and then veer right off its end (see the map).

However let's take the convoluted route. From Lough Firrib head down the spur for about 10 minutes and then swing north-east downhill off it. If you find the terrain too steep or craggy veer left into easier ground. On this course you should eventually reach the flat bottom of the valley mentioned above, at this point with trees on the other side of its main stream. Turn left to walk downstream.

This is a lovely stretch, with hills rising on both sides and generally moderately good ground underfoot. You will have to cross the river eventually so perhaps the best place is where forest ends on the far bank. After that you will pass by a few low waterfalls and eventually come under the rocky nose of Fair Mountain on the right. Continue downstream between trees set back from the river bank, another lovely section. This will take you down to the sizeable King's River, where you turn right upstream. In a hundred metres or so the river swings at right angles right (in its direction of flow of course) and just beyond this you will come to a small tributary that meets the main river at right angles (it's a fluvially right angle type of area). If you have any residual doubt about your location you will hardly miss the two sets of monstrous lines just ahead.

The idea now is simply to follow this tributary upstream to its source. This will take you under the cliffs of Fair Mountain on the right and, I hate to have to say this, right along the route of, and close to, the electricity lines. You may initially have to hop from one side of the tributary to the other to avoid clumps of forest but farther up you are in a valley and can make rapid progress.

At length you will reach an all too prominent electricity station. From it take a narrow concrete road the short distance to the start. ■

ROUTE 24: CIRCUIT OF GLENBRIDE

Starting at a remote location this route reaches Mullaghcleevaun, the second-highest peak in Wicklow, on a satisfying circuit. Before and after there is expansive moorland, wet normally but almost a quagmire in places after rain. Mercifully, little forestry.

Getting There There are several ways of reaching the start from Dublin. One way is to take the N81 past *Blessington*, shortly after turn left onto the R758, fork right beyond Valleymount to keep on the R758, at its end turn left onto the R756, turn left onto a side road after 3 miles, turn first right (signed cul-de-sac) and park at the forest entrance on the left after a half-mile. You can also reach the start from the *Wicklow Gap* direction, taking the first tarmac road right after the Gap, the first for miles, and first right again, the cul-de-sac road.

Walking Time 5 hours (distance 13.6km, climb 720m).

Difficulties Lots of wet, boggy terrain. With few distinct features, navigation is generally difficult but with no cliffs and few areas of forest in the area, mistakes should not be serious.

Map Sheet 56. The Glendalough Glenmalur 1:25 000 map shows the more complicated southern part of the route, but not the simpler northern.

Route From the forest entrance walk onward (east) along the road for a few hundred metres until the forest border, at first close on the left and then farther away, swings away directly uphill. Around here cross a gate on the left into rough pasture to start the climb to the top of Silsean.

There is no navigational problem about this climb: keep the forestry fence on the left. It extends way above the top of the forest into extensive moorland. Where it finally finishes, at the meeting of two fences at an acute angle, the summit is only a short distance to the west.

Silsean (698m), high but unimpressive, has a boggy summit plateau, in parts of which lie a flotilla of shallow pools. The views encompass the broad expanse of Pollaphuca Reservoir and a wide range of mountain including the ultimate goal of the route, imposing Mullaghcleevaun off to the east.

From Silsean walk north-east towards Moanbane. At the shallow col between the two mountains you may like to take a break; the hags here offer the only sheltered spot you are likely to find in the long stretch to Mullaghcleevaun. After which, climb to the summit of Moanbane (703m), like its sister, Silsean, a boggy plateau with only a few tiny lakes to relieve its monotony.

The next stretch is across an extensive area of moorland: east from Moanbane to Billy Byrne's Gap, which is about a kilometre away and then gently uphill north-east for about another kilometre. You then swing east to begin the assault on Mullaghcleevaun, probably skirting a distinct area of peat hags in the flat ground at the beginning of this leg, a minor navigational aid.

Once you start the real climb to the summit of Mullaghcleevaun the underfoot conditions change radically. It's not only much steeper, but the ground is dry with occasional boulders. The summit plateau (849m, 3.25 hours) has a trig pillar that serves as its focus; a little farther north-east, overlooking the corrie cradling Lough Ouler, is a memorial to three An Oige members who died in a boating accident in the fifties. As for the views, they are not as good as one might reasonably expect from such a high position. The high ridge running southward culminating in Tonelagee is the most impressive, with the north-eastern and western spurs, both of which terminate here, being more subdued.

A compass bearing of 210° will take you onto the spur running south with a touch of west from Tonelagee, as opposed to south with a touch of east which would take you along the Barnacullian ridge towards Tonelagee, and so onto a

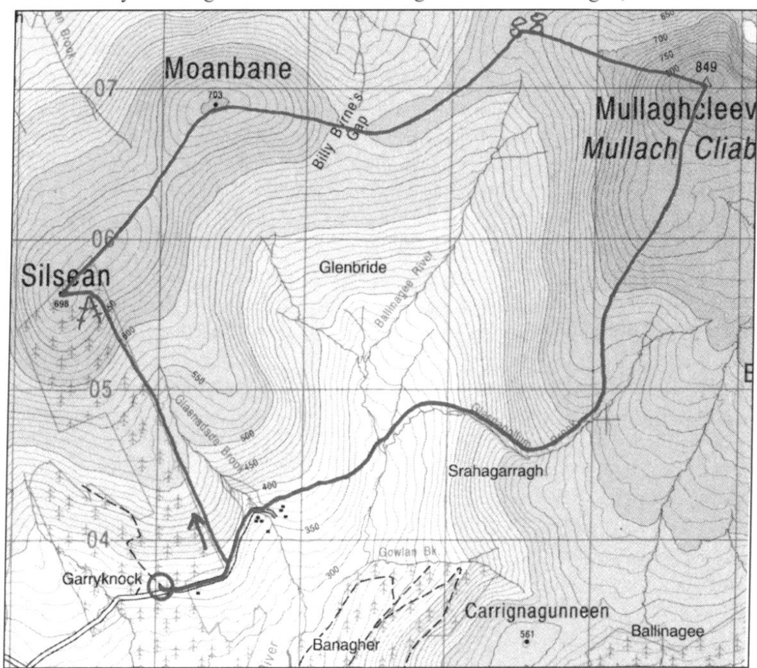

similar but incorrect spur. This (correct) direction takes you along an area of grass sliced by parallel indentations and then through forlorn decaying peat hags crouching feebly in a muddy brown sea – all a little surreal. Continuing south you will enter the upper valley of the Glasnagollum Brook, here flowing south-west. Like nearly all such mountain streams in Wicklow, this is a lovely stretch giving easy walking and is of course navigationally child's play.

As you approach Glenbride's bottom you should see a rough track on the other side of the main stream in the valley, the Ballinagee River. Cross this stream to reach the track and turn left uphill onto it. This will take you west between cultivated ground bounded by stone walls and eventually (a short eventually) into the hamlet of Glenbride. Continue on through the hamlet, crossing its bridge to reach tarmac. The start is about a kilometre farther on.

Variations This is an exceptionally good area for variations, both shorter and longer. For instance you can descend into Glenbride from Billy Byrne's Gap, walk to Barnacullian or descend into Glenbride from the forest west of Carrignagunneen (which is not worth climbing). ■

ROUTE 25: MULLAGHCLEEVAUN FROM THE NORTH

An area of abundant gently sloping moorland does not at first seem very inviting. However the initial walk along the banks of a stream slicing through that moorland and the wide views from the high centre section more than compensate for the dull country around Black Hill. A surprisingly varied route.

Getting There From Dublin there are two possible routes. The shorter is to take the N81 towards *Blessington*, turn left off it onto the R759 just after Brittas, follow signs for Sally Gap for over 4 miles to turn right (signed 'Blessington 6') to cross the River Liffey. Turn first left (set your milometer here), ignore the cul-de-sac road on the left and park at a forest entrance at 2.1 miles (the second of two closely spaced entrances on the left) (GR 058118). The road is extremely narrow for the last few miles. Alternatively drive to *Lackan,* fork left here to park in the carpark at Ballynultagh Gap (GR 044108). The route commentary then starts at the last paragraph of the route description.

Walking Time 5.5 hours (distance 16km, climb 580m), which allows about 15 minutes over Naismith for slow progress along a river bank.

Difficulties Near the start you must ford a river that may be difficult after rain; there is much soft ground and a few points requiring careful navigation.

Map Sheet 56.

Route Take the narrow road into forest (not the forest track on its right). Emerging from forest at a tee, take the left branch and just before the 'temporary' dwelling, beyond which is a farmhouse, turn right off the track and head generally south through abandoned fields to reach the valley's main stream, Ballydonnell Brook.

Shortly after reaching the Brook you will come to a fence corner beyond which are young trees. From this corner walk upstream for another few minutes until you come to a major tributary (it's Lugaculleen Brook). Cross Ballydonnell Brook here (you may have to go some distance upstream) and follow Lugaculleen Brook to its source, which it does without gathering any major tributary, a fact which greatly simplifies navigation. You will pass some deciduous trees on the south-west bank at a narrow cleft shortly after leaving Ballydonnell Brook; otherwise there are no major features until you come to an area that looks like a field at about GR 084085, with steep, rocky slopes rising behind it. The steep, rocky, slopes are real enough, but the 'field' is only a reedy low-lying area.

From the 'field' climb steeply south-east to the left of scattered crags and so reach high ground, Duff Hill to the east, Mullaghcleevaun East Top to the south-west and, at this point only of academic interest, the rim of the corrie holding Cleevaun Lough the main feature to the west.

The East Top is the next goal. Note that it has two tops, both to be climbed: the first has a cairn on a boulder, the higher top (795m), 400m to the south has a cairn on flat ground with lots of tastefully disposed boulders scattered around it. From East Top the climb to Mullaghcleevaun is easy, though you may want to swing right of the direct line to avoid a slough of black mud in the shallow col.

Mullaghcleevaun (847m, 3.25 hours), (briefly described under route 24) has a trig pillar which makes it unmistakable. From the summit it's worthwhile walking north to the corrie edge to look down into Cleevaun Lough.

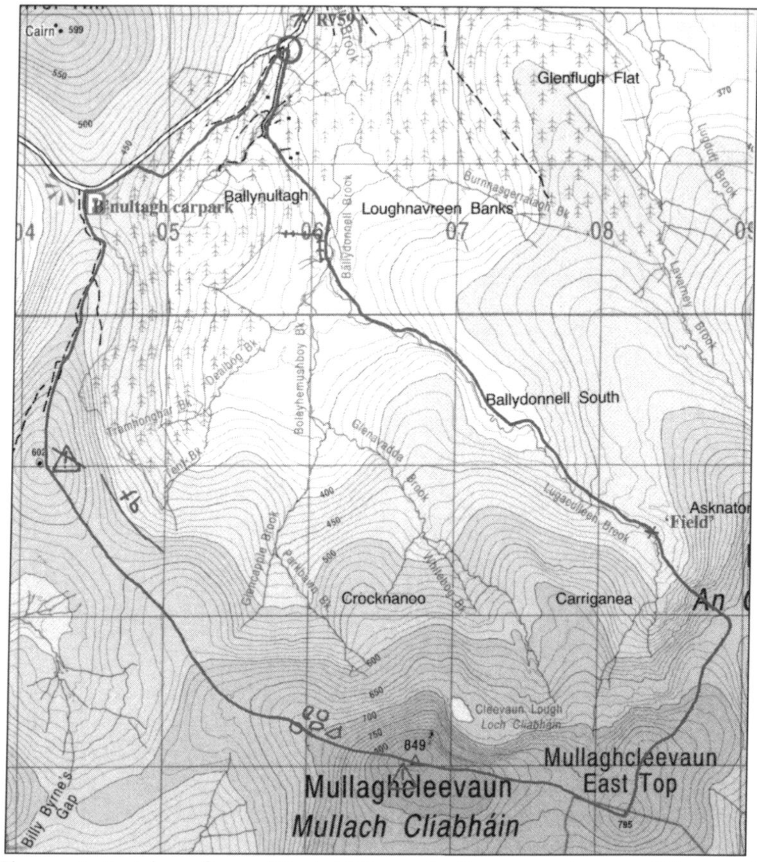

The next stretch as far as Black Hill nearly 4km away is one of the most featureless in Wicklow. This means attention to navigation, though there are no hazards apart from, as you leave the summit, the cliffs over the Cleevaun Lough corrie. A compass bearing of 300 will ensure you miss these and instead take you steeply downhill to cross a compact and distinct region of hags, and so of some help in navigation. Then, keeping a broad firebreak off to the right, cross a soggy plain and ascend the soggy slopes of Black Hill to finally arrive at its soggy summit (602m).

With sogginess now thankfully behind walk north from Black Hill to pick up a bog track. This takes you to the carpark at Ballynultagh Gap. From the Gap turn right to walk along the road, crossing the first gate on the right– it's set back – after a few hundred metres. Take the wide grassy firebreak beyond through scattered trees to a forest track. Turn left onto it and walk the kilometre or so straight back to the start. ■

ROUTE 26: SLIEVECORRAGH AND CHURCH MOUNTAIN

A walk through pleasant agricultural lowlands, as well as gently sloped mountain and moorland with wide views especially over the plains to the west.

Getting There Take the N81 past *Blessington* to turn left after about 6 miles onto the R756. Take the second turn left to park in the village of Hollywood (GR 9405).

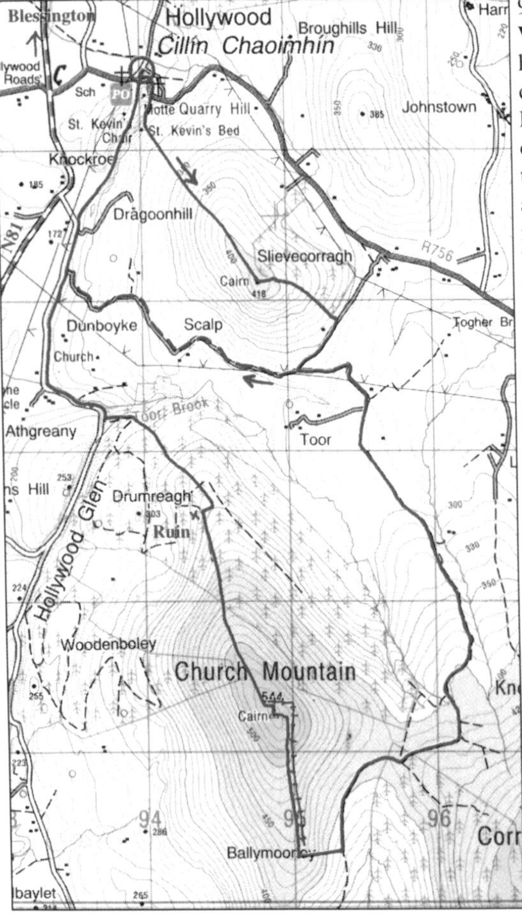

Walking Time 4.75 hours (distance 14km, climb 600m).

Difficulties There is a lot of bracken on parts of this route so it might be advisable to avoid it in mid and late summer. Navigation is easy.

Map Sheet 56.

Route From the village walk back to the R756, turn left and cross the first gate on the right to reach a grassy track giving good views over the lowlands to the west and, right below you, an impressive glacial channel (1). After only a few minutes you will reach a statue of St Kevin (so they say, but it looks more like a recycled St Patrick to me) and you can here start your climb to the summit of Slievecorragh (418m) to the south-east.

The summit, marked by a few ruins, is easily reached but the descent is decidedly more difficult because of fences and, lower down, enclosed fields bordering the road. Walk east from the summit for a few metres until you meet a fence running roughly south-east to mature forest below, and if you keep this forest close on the left you will easily reach a narrow road.

Turn right onto it and take it to a tee close to a huge set of pylons, where you should turn sharply left. The road turns at right angles to the right and after it, and you are now facing south, you should continue roughly in this direction, mostly on a track heading gradually upward into moorland for all of 2km.

The track eventually levels out with the dome of Corriebracks to the south-east and Church Mountain rising much more prominently to the west, its near side corrugated by lines of ditches for forestry. In the complex network of tracks going every which way hereabouts it should still be little trouble to find the one that takes you southwards along the flank of Church on the right with a wide forested valley on the left. Walk down this track to a gate and cross it. Turn immediately right to start the climb to the crest of the summit's long southern spur and having attained it (the spur) turn right to follow a firebreak and forestry fence leading almost to the summit. If you care to leave the firebreak and walk a little to the west you will be rewarded by long views over the plains of Kildare.

To reach the summit (544m, 3.25 hours) you will have to divert from the firebreak and walk a few metres to a huge heap of stones that makes the trig pillar look quite inadequate. In an area of generally undistinguished peaks this is one you will not mistake!

The descent requires a little care to get onto the correct route. From the heap of stones, walk a few metres north to a fence, turn left at it and where there is shortly a break in the fence turn right (north) to walk down what will later transpire to be a firebreak. This is confirmed farther down where mature forest closes in on the left and not so mature forest does likewise on the right.

Where the firebreak eventually levels off at a ruin turn right to reach a nearby gate at the end of a track in a partly felled area. Take this track downhill, and ignore a steeply rising track on the left to reach a nearby forest entrance. Turn right here onto tarmac. There's now over a kilometre of quiet country road ahead. When you swing sharply left around a house and see a STOP sign ahead at the main road, the N81, cross a gate on the right to follow a rough track north through the curious grassy hummocks left by the glacial spillway. This track will take you all the way back to Hollywood.

An Exceptionally Short Variation This takes in Slievecorragh and little more. Take the main route above to its summit and down to the road beyond. Turn right onto this road (as above) but turn right where the main route shortly turns left. This will take you for about 2km along a winding, undulating narrow lane running through agricultural country. At its end turn right onto the 'main road' and look out for the STOP sign ahead that marks the return to the main route. Walking time is about 2 hours (distance 6km, climb 250m).

Note

(1) Glacial Spillways. At the end of the last ice age there was a great lake to the north of here hemmed in by ice sheets and the surrounding hills. As the rising temperatures caused the ice to melt the lake waters rose and eventually spilt out, in a great torrent, over the lowest point in the impounding hills. What's to be seen now is the channel for this flood of water, a glacial spillway. There's an even more impressive example at the Scalp on the other side of the mountains. ■

ROUTE 27: LUGNAQUILLIA AND THE UPPER GLEN OF IMAAL

A long and lovely walk, much of it over high ground with expansive views over impressive mountain scenery. Underfoot conditions are generally good. Because of the proximity of the Artillery Range not a route that can be easily shortened.

Getting There Drive to *Donard*, and continue straight ahead in the village to pass the youth hostel. About 1.6 miles beyond it park at the forest entrance on the left with a junction opposite it. There is ample space here for carefully parked cars (GR 983948). You can also park at Fenton's pub further south (GR 973935).

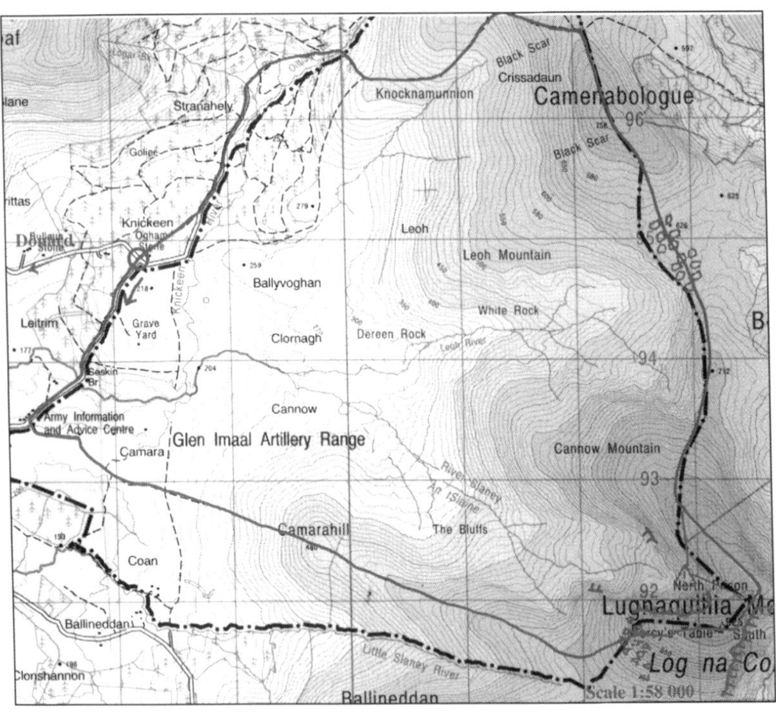

Walking Time 6.25 hours (distance 19km, climb 900m).

Difficulties There are paths for most of the way but do not rely on them to do the navigation for you. In particular, careful navigation is required on the descent from Lugnaquillia. Except in an emergency, you are committed to the route from beyond its summit because of the need to keep clear of the Artillery Range. Note that though the route to Lugnaquillia passes through the Range (as shown on the maps) it is still okay to walk it unless red flags are flying on the approach roads. The Range Warden Service (☎ 045-404653) has further information.

Map Sheet 56. The eastern (upland) part of the route is on the Glendalough Glenmalur 1:25 000 map.

Route Take the road south for less than 2km to pass Fenton's pub. Turn left just beyond it and walk onward over an extremely rutted road, which soon becomes a track complete with formidable pools of water. At a crosstracks continue straight ahead on a grassy track running up the face of Camarahill.

This track lasts for only a few hundred metres, but an earthbank will guide you all the way to the summit (480m) and beyond it for 100m or so on a short downhill, the one and only this side of Lug. Pass a heap of rocks and then start the climb to Lugnaquillia in earnest on a rough but continuous path.

This is a lovely stretch, the cliffs of the North Prison ahead, the Ballineddan spur approaching from the right and the great unforested expanse of the Artillery Range down on the left. Navigation is easy: just follow the rough path which runs generally east to expire temporarily at steeper boulder-strewn ground close to Lug. On the short grass of the summit plateau the path resumes and continues to the great summit cairn itself. Lugnaquillia (925m, 3.25 hours) is described under route 12. Suffice to say here that it gives a marvellous view over splendid mountain scenery.

The descent requires a little care, the general idea being to reach the summit of Camenabologue (GR 0295) 4km to the north. In bad visibility take a bearing of 52° compass for 350m or so and then swing to 324° for about 800m, taking care at the end of this leg not to walk too far onto the beguiling grassy shoulder of Cannow. Instead swing right, keeping to the high ground and picking up a prominent path which will ensure that you do not wander east onto the plentiful peat hags on Benleagh (689m) and pt 663m.

The path leads down a rocky spur with a whole galaxy of peaks ahead: the great hump of Tonelagee beyond the pumped storage reservoir, muted Mullaghcleevaun further away to its left and even the tip of Great Sugar Loaf. And not only peaks, for there are marvellous views into Glenmalure and beyond Fraughan Rock Glen to lofty Art's Lough, tucked in under the cliffs of Clohernagh.

The lower ground just south of Camenabologue is soggy, with peat hags, after which there is a steep climb of about 150m to the summit (758m), crowned by an imposing cairn, the first major one since Lug. From Camenabologue it is a short and pleasant walk downhill through the occasional peat hag, strangely standing in quite dry ground, to the top of the pass (at GR 0296) between Glen of Imaal and Glenmalure, which offers a sheltered little nook for grub.

The rest of the route, waymarked path or track all the way, is that approved by the Army authorities and is easy to describe and indeed walk. Sadly, after the splendours of the route so far, it is a little monotonous. From the pass start off downhill to the west taking not the better grassy track running north-west, but the initially more indistinct track on its left. Continue downhill until Army waymarks divert you right off the track, past skeletons of trees on the left and across two adjacent footbridges. These lead to a nearby forest track, later a rutted road, which should be followed until you are diverted right off this, back onto a forest track for the last few hundred metres. ■

ROUTE 28: THE ASBAWN AND GLENREEMORE BROOKS

The Asbawn to be followed uphill, the Glenreemore downhill, the latter in particularly splendid surrounds. Between these the route visits the small lakes sheltering in the austere boglands of the high mountains. Though navigation is in parts not easy, this is an area with few hazards; the route can be easily varied.

Getting There Take the N81 past *Blessington* to turn left onto the R756. Follow this road for 3 miles; where it swings sharply left continue straight ahead for another 3 miles. At this point the road, never better than mediocre, crosses over a bridge and definitely becomes a track. Continue onward, braving suspension damage, for a few more hundred metres to park on waste ground on the right (GR 016014). The total distance from Dublin is 31 miles.

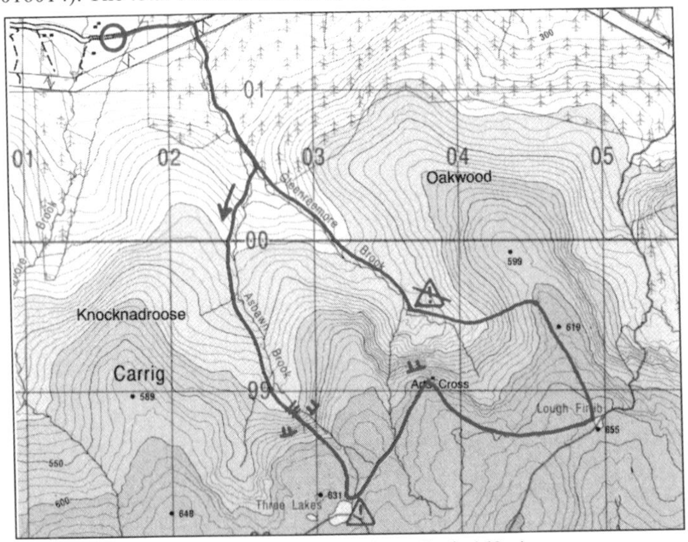

Walking Time 3.75 hours (distance 11km, climb 460m).

Difficulties Navigation on the moorland that forms much of this route is difficult in bad visibility. However there are no more than short stretches of cliff in the area, so mistakes should not be disastrous.

Map Sheet 56 or the Glendalough Glenmalur 1:25 000 map.

Route Walk a few hundred metres farther along the track to pass through a gate. Turn right just beyond it to cross a rough bridge over the Glenreemore Brook and pass under the giant electricity pylons from Turlough Hill. You are now in an unplanted area between two blocks of forest (incidentally, it is shown as forest on sheet 56), with the swirling Glenreemore Brook on the right. After a few hundred metres of mild but steady climbing, of which there is much on this route, you will find the forest edge swinging away on the right. A little farther on, and before forest swings away in turn on the left, take the right fork at a major confluence, thus following the Asbawn Brook.

But before setting off from this junction, a word about the topography. There is an impressive valley on the left, the one drained by the Glenreemore, which we will be walking down later in the day. The spur on this valley's right, a rocky one, is topped by Art's Cross, which should be visible from about here; we will be visiting it later. Before all this however, we will be following the Asbawn Brook to its source.

This involves an easy climb through bogland with only one slightly worrying tributary, one flowing in from the right, and *not* to be followed. Just keep the high ground close on the left all the way up and follow the appropriate tributary. You will thus reach the end of the shallowly sloped uplands drained by the Asbawn and face the only real climb of the day.

This climb, among modest crags, is south-east following the Asbawn, which at one point descends in a low waterfall. Where the ground levels out you are in a world much different to that lower down: the bogland of the higher hills, a world of peat hags, bog cotton and undulating soggy moorland. Continue directly south on almost level ground, still following a stream (make sure it is flowing north, though) and in a few hundred metres you will reach the larger (yes, there are only two) of the lakes of Three Lakes (1.75 hours).

From here on, in bad visibility at least, you are into map and compass territory. Walk north-east to Art's Cross, about 1km away over the bogland. Art's Cross, while it has no great pretensions in the pulchritude stakes, is visible from afar and thus has one great advantage over the next target, Lough Firrib, which is notoriously difficult to find in poor visibility, and not all that easy in good.

There is a path for the first part of the leg to the lake giving easy walking. However it fades away and does not necessarily abandon the walker on the direct line from Cross to lake. It might, therefore be prudent in bad conditions to ignore the path and follow a compass bearing of 114° all the way over bogland (yes, more of it), bordering the valleys and spurs to the north.

Lough Firrib is a small heart-shaped lake backed on the south by exceptionally soft ground. From it yet another compass bearing (this time 348°) is advisable to take you north-west along the Oakwood spur: it is apparent enough when you get onto it but far from so on the first few hundred metres from the lough. Once you reach it keep to the crest for less than a kilometre and then drop left (west) off it to reach a remote basin near the source of the Glenreemore Brook — or a little downstream from it. This descent requires a little care to avoid high heather and rocks. To avoid the worst, do not head down too soon.

Once you reach the valley floor the rest is navigationally easy and the walk along the fast-flowing Glenreemore Brook is delightful. This is true especially of the first part, where the rocky spur on the left of the valley is most impressive. At length you will reach forest, first on the right, then on both sides. (Let's hope you recognise it – you should since you toiled upwards here at the start of the route.) The forest will now funnel you across the bridge crossed earlier. After it turn left onto a track to reach the nearby start.

Variations You can lengthen this route by adding in Conavalla or by walking from Lough Firrib into the valley to the east close to Fair Mountain and then following the forest edge east into Glenreemore. You can easily shorten it by heading down to Glenreemore from Art's Cross (but take care to avoid crags on the initial descent). ■

ROUTE 29: BALLINEDDAN AND CAMARAHILL

Good ground underfoot and lovely long views on a short walk taking in three not very distinguished peaks. The walk can easily be extended to include Lugnaquillia, thus adding one memorable summit to the day.

Getting There Drive to *Donard*, keep straight ahead here to pass the youth hostel, shortly turn right to keep on the main road, pass through the crossroads at Knockanarrigan, so following a sign for Aughavannagh. Less than a half-mile farther on do *not* turn right to pass over a bridge. Instead, continue straight ahead for nearly 2 miles to park at an Army warning notice on the left fronting a track (GR 986914). The total distance from Dublin is 37 miles.

You can also start the walk at Fenton's pub (GR 973935), thus (maybe) reducing the car journey at the expense of increasing the track walk. You can then take a track directly from here to the crosstrack mentioned at the end of the route description.

Walking Time 3.25 hours (distance 9km, climb 560m). The extension of the route to Lugnaquillia (see below) will take an additional 1.25 hours (3km distance and 240m climb extra).

Difficulties Navigation and underfooot conditions are easy. There are stepping stones to cross at the very end of the route, when wet feet, if it comes to that, should not be too uncomfortable. If you are worried about them walk a few metres up the track mentioned above before you set out and you will be able to judge their difficulty.

Map Sheet 56 with much of the higher ground also on the Glendalough Glenmalur 1:25 000 map. Make sure you do not get lost southwards; if you think you will, take sheet 62 as a precaution!

Route Walk onward (south-east) along the road for a few hundred metres, here crossing a double gate on the left with several scenic ruins beyond it. Follow the rutted track past the ruins and through another gate, where surprisingly the track improves. In spite of this, you must leave it around here and head south-east towards nearby forest clothing the lower slopes of Ballineddan, the first summit.

Near the forest head cross a stile and then head directly upward east following an earthbank which runs nearly to the top, a steep ascent over easy ground. The summit (652m) consists of a grassy mound, as said before undistinguished, but with bulky Keadeen to the west, the sharp outline of the Brusselstown Ring to its right and the Glen of Imaal at your feet, to say nothing of the massing hills to its (the Glen's) north and east, this is a great viewpoint.

From Ballineddan continue east over short grass to Slievemaan, passing an outcrop on the way, an odd sight in an otherwise grassy terrain. Lofty Slievemaan (759m, 2 hours), its summit much wetter than Ballineddan's, also gives excellent views. You cannot fail to be impressed by the great block of Lugnaquillia to the north-east, but note also the long spur reaching away north-west from it (Lug) and here well below you. This is the Camarahill spur, of which much anon.

From Slievemaan head north-east towards Lug, passing through peat hags on the way down and an area of mud at the col facing it. Here a decision point: you can elect climb to Lugnaquillia or you can head directly to the Camarahill spur. If you have the time and you have never been there it hardly needs saying that the variation to Lugnaquillia is well worth taking. The ascent is sustained and fairly steep; from the huge summit cairn head west to descend on the Camarahill spur.

However let's stick with the main route. From the col contour north-west for about 500m to reach the Camarahill spur. There is a path along the crest of the spur but in bad conditions use map and compass rather than relying on finding it. Once on the spur the rest is easy. Keep walking west and gently downhill along a partly muddy path. This is a lovely stretch though the best of it is behind towards the great cliffs of the North Prison. Don't wander right on this spur: to the north is the Artillery Range and is so strictly off limits.

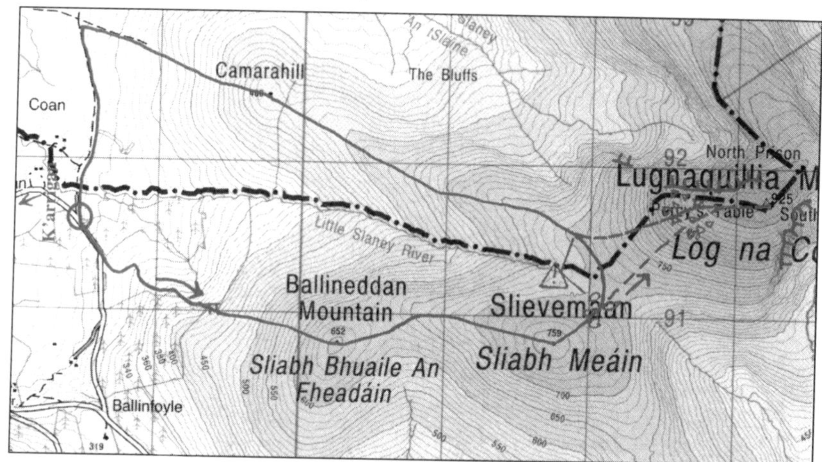

After two kilometres or so along the spur you will come to an area of rocks, a change from the grassy ground up to this. Beyond is a slight climb, the first since Slievemaan. This is the only indication of Camarahill (480m), moderately impressive from the Glen of Imaal but not much here in the company of loftier and far more impressive peaks.

From Camarahill continue west downhill shortly following an earthbank. Cross a high stile and follow the track beyond to a crosstracks. Turn left here to walk over a kilometre to the stepping stones mentioned above. This is the Little Slaney River. It usually matches its epithet but if it is in flood and doesn't there is nothing for it but wet feet to end. ■

ROUTE 30: KEADEEN AND CARRIG

Keadeen (653m), a bulky but none too shapely peak, commands excellent long views over the plains of Kildare and far beyond from its isolated position at the edge of the range. The climb to its southern outlier Carrig, a peak even less shapely than Keadeen, along with some track and road walking, makes a circuit out of what would otherwise be a there and back.

Getting There The total distance from Dublin is 38 miles. One of several ways of getting there is to drive to *Donard*, continue onward past the youth hostel, shortly turn first right to Knockarrigan, continue straight ahead, now following the signs for the Dwyer-McAllister cottage. Drive past the Cottage, fork right and park shortly at the forest entrance where forest ceases on the right but continues on the left (GR 984895). There is room here for several cars.

Walking Time 3.75 hours (distance 10km, climb 560m).

Difficulties Some navigational uncertainty in the farmland east of Carrig, but there is no dangerous terrain anywhere in the area.

Map Sheet 62.

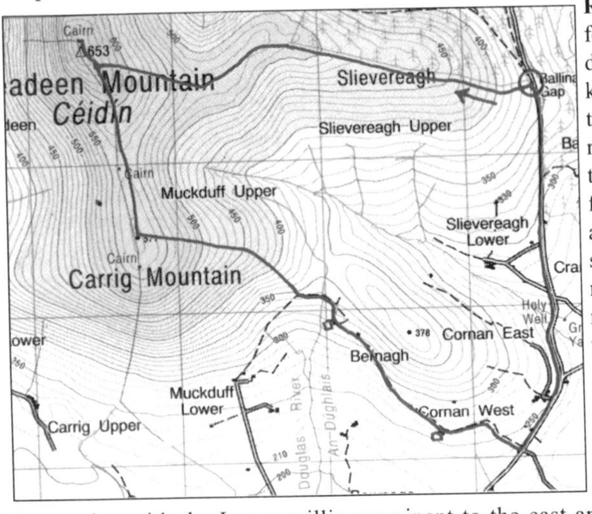

Route From the forest entrance walk directly uphill keeping the edge of the forest on the right. At the top of the forest you can follow a rutted track all the way to the summit, veering right at the summit ridge to reach the trig pillar and a mighty heap of stones, described simply as a cairn on the OS map. The views are most impressive with the Lugnaquillia prominent to the east and a wide range of agricultural land reaching out to the west. One feature that you might look out for are the walls lopsidedly circling the Brusselstown Ring to the north-west; the summit of Keadeen must be the one place from which you can appreciate their full magnitude.

From the summit head south following a fence to the shallow col facing Carrig and climb the short distance to the summit cairn (571m), which is just south of the vague summit itself. From here walk east along the crest of the broad spur reaching into agricultural land and when you near upland fields prepare mentally for navigational headaches, but it has to be said, also most attractive, varied, upland agricultural scenery.

The idea is to reach a track traversing fields to the right of the spur by veering off it (the crest) before the point where upland fields clothe it (the crest again). On